Intelligent Business

Teacher's Book

Intermediate
Business English

| Louise Pile | Susan Lowe |

Pearson Education Limited
Edinburgh Gate
Harlow
Essex CM20 2JE
England
and Associated Companies throughout the world.

www.pearsonelt.com

© Pearson Education Limited 2005

The right of Louise Pile and Susan Lowe to be identified as authors of this Work has been asserted by them in accordance with the Copyright, Designs and Patents Act 1988.

All rights reserved; no part of this publication may be reproduced, stored in a retrieval system, or transmitted in any form or by any means, electronic, mechanical, photocopying, recording, or otherwise without the prior written permission of the Publishers.

First published 2005
Ninth impression 2016

ISBN: 978-0-582-84798-9 (Int Bus Inter TBK fr pk)

ISBN: 978-1-4058-4314-0 (Int Bus Int TM CD-ROM fr pk)

ISBN: 978-1-4058-4340-9 (Int Bus Int TBK/TM CD-Rom Pack)

Set in Times New Roman 10/12

Printed and bound by CPI Group (UK) Ltd, Croydon, CR0 4YY

Acknowledgements

The publishers are grateful to The Economist for permission to adapt copyright material on page 117 (©2004) and to use Economist texts as a source of background information.

All material copyright of The Economist Newspaper Limited.

All rights reserved.

The authors would like to thank the editor Anne Williams for her help in developing this book.

Designed by Wooden Ark

Contents

Page
4   **Introduction**

15	**Coursebook: Teacher's notes**
104	**Coursebook glossary test: Answers**
105	**Coursebook review: Answers**
108	**Coursebook: Photocopiable resources**

      1.1: email recommendation framework
      1.2: Company profile
      2.1: Card activity (collocations)
      2.2: Card activity (getting things done)
      3.1: Written recommendations
      4.1: Flexible benefits
      5.1: Prioritisation of development issues
      5.2: Development project plan
      6.1: Planning a trade fair
      7.1: Card activity (conditional dialogues)
      7.2: Card activity (conditional questions)
      8.1: Card activity (financial vocabulary)
      10.1: Card activity (opposites / prefixes)
      8.2: Card activity (report writing phrases)
      9.1: Dos and Don'ts of CV writing
      11.1: e-commerce website evaluation
      12.1: Card activity (lobbying collocations)
      13.1: Card activity (voicemail scenarios)
      14.1: Card activity (passives)

121	**Skills Book: Teacher's notes**
176	**Skills Book: Photocopiable resources**

      1.1: Card activity (talking about your job)
      1.2: Card activity (present tenses)
      2.1: Planning for a deadline
      4.1: Present perfect / past simple questionnaire
      6.1: Card activity (comparatives and superlatives)
      7.1: Tentative suggestions
      8.1: Card activity (language of change)
      9.1: Domino card activity (questions)
      9.2: Card activity (socialising)
      11.1: Card activity (gerund or infinitive)
      13.1: Card activity (reported speech)
      13.2: Card activity (meeting)
      14.1: Questions following a presentation
      15.1: Negotiation planner

185	**Photocopiable frameworks**

INTELLIGENT BUSINESS (INTERMEDIATE) TEACHER'S BOOK

Introduction

Rationale

Today, the demand for Business English is greater than ever. And with the increasingly globalised world of international business, it looks set to keep on growing. As a result, the teaching and learning of Business English is playing an increasingly important role in business studies and everyday corporate life. Although the need for Business English is the same for students at a business school as it is for employees in a company, their needs and learning circumstances are very different.

For students at a business school, the main challenge is often understanding business itself, not only the English language. Fortunately, the tertiary education environment usually provides enough classroom hours to deal with these challenges. For students studying business full time, the key is to *learn business* through the medium of the English language.

For people already active in the workplace and with some understanding of the world of business, often the challenge is finding the time to learn Business English. Furthermore, for managers with a very good business knowledge, their learning experience must reflect this understanding of business practices and reality. For these students language learning is not an academic exercise but a need to translate familiar business practices into English as quickly as possible. Here the key is to *do business* in English.

Intelligent Business is a range of Business English materials that includes components specifically designed to meet the needs of students who either need to *learn business through English* or *perform familiar business tasks in English*. These materials can be used individually or, as they share a core language and skills syllabus, can be used in a variety of combinations described later in this introduction. For an overview of all the *Intelligent Business Intermediate* components, please see fig. 1.

As well as sharing a common demand for Business English, both institutional and corporate learning environments are experiencing an increased demand for measurability. Today, both course tutors and training managers are under increasing pressure to measure and demonstrate progress and a return on the investment in Business English learning activities. As this is most effectively done using external, standardised and globally recognised examinations, *Intelligent Business Intermediate* is benchmarked against the Cambridge Business English Certificate (BEC) Vantage level.

Finally, any Business English materials today need to draw on authentic sources and achieve a high degree of validity in the eyes of the learners and teachers who use them. Developed in collaboration with *The Economist* magazine, *Intelligent Business* draws on this rich source of authoritative and topical articles on the business world.

INTRODUCTION

Fig. 1

Coursebook
StyleGuide
Audio CDs

Workbook
Audio CD

Teacher's Book

Skills Book
CDROM

Video Resource Book
Video

Website
Premium content,
Teacher's Resources,
Review Tests,
BEC Exam Practice

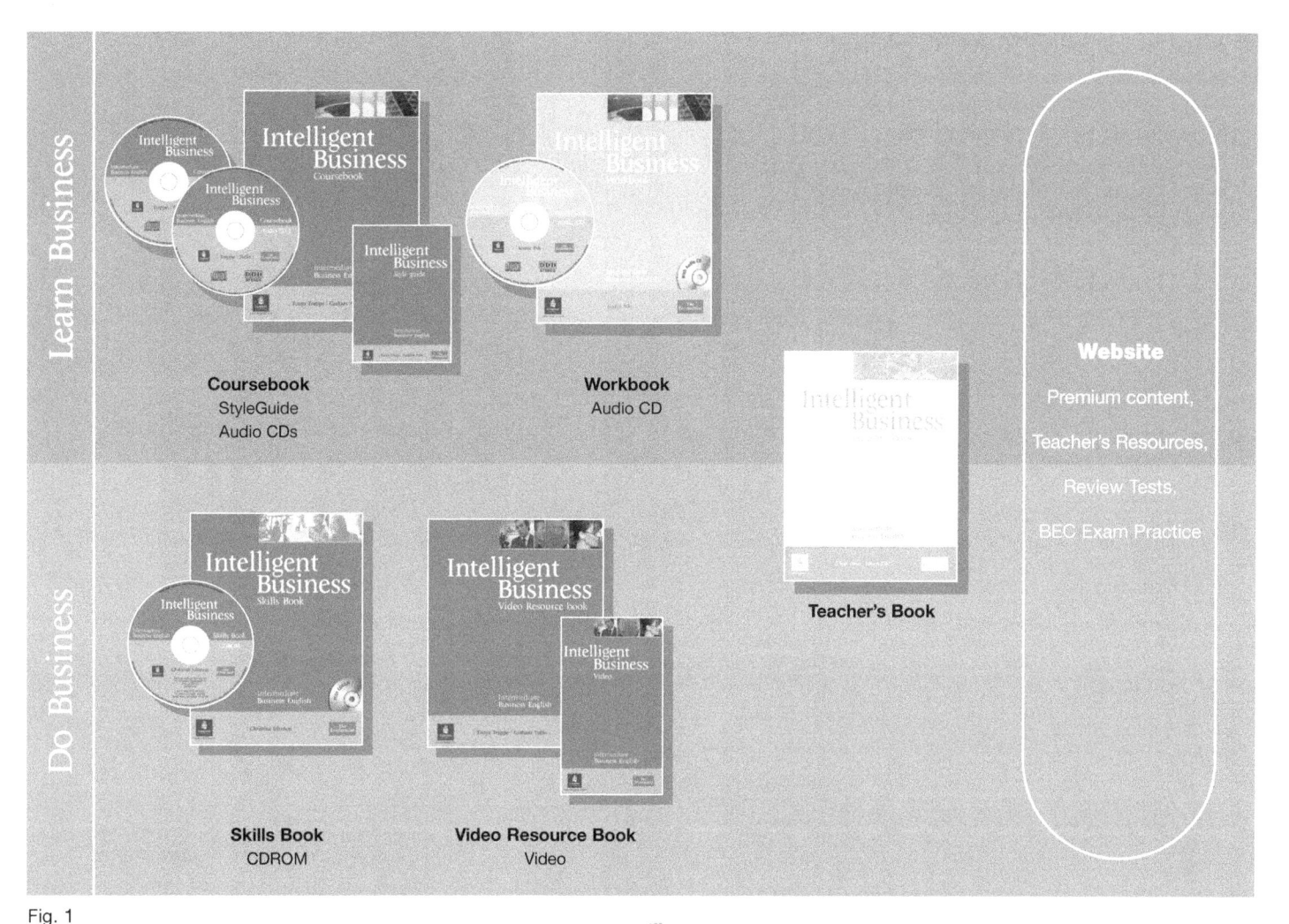

Learn Business

Learn Business refers to the components designed to be especially accessible to learners who may not have much business experience or knowledge. These components include the *Intelligent Business* Coursebook and Workbook. The Coursebook provides 100+ hours of classroom-based teaching material divided into fifteen units. The course is built on an intermediate grammar syllabus and uses plenty of authentic text to present grammar and vocabulary that is then extracted and practised in isolation. The texts are benchmarked against the word limits found at Cambridge BEC Vantage.

The Coursebook also includes a *Career Skills* syllabus that develops key communicative skills to help people within any kind of organisational – not just a corporate – environment. These communicative skills are supplemented by a *Culture at Work* feature that raises students' awareness of how cultural differences can affect communication between people of different nationalities.

In addition, the Coursebook includes *Dilemma and Decision* (case study-style problem-solving activities) and regular reviews. These are designed to review the key grammar and functional language developed within the unit.

5

INTELLIGENT BUSINESS (INTERMEDIATE) TEACHER'S BOOK

At the back of the book there is a grammar reference, a glossary with test and a *Style Guide* – a pocket-sized 32-page booklet providing support on common forms of business correspondence such as email, letters and memos, along with general notes on organisation, style and accuracy.

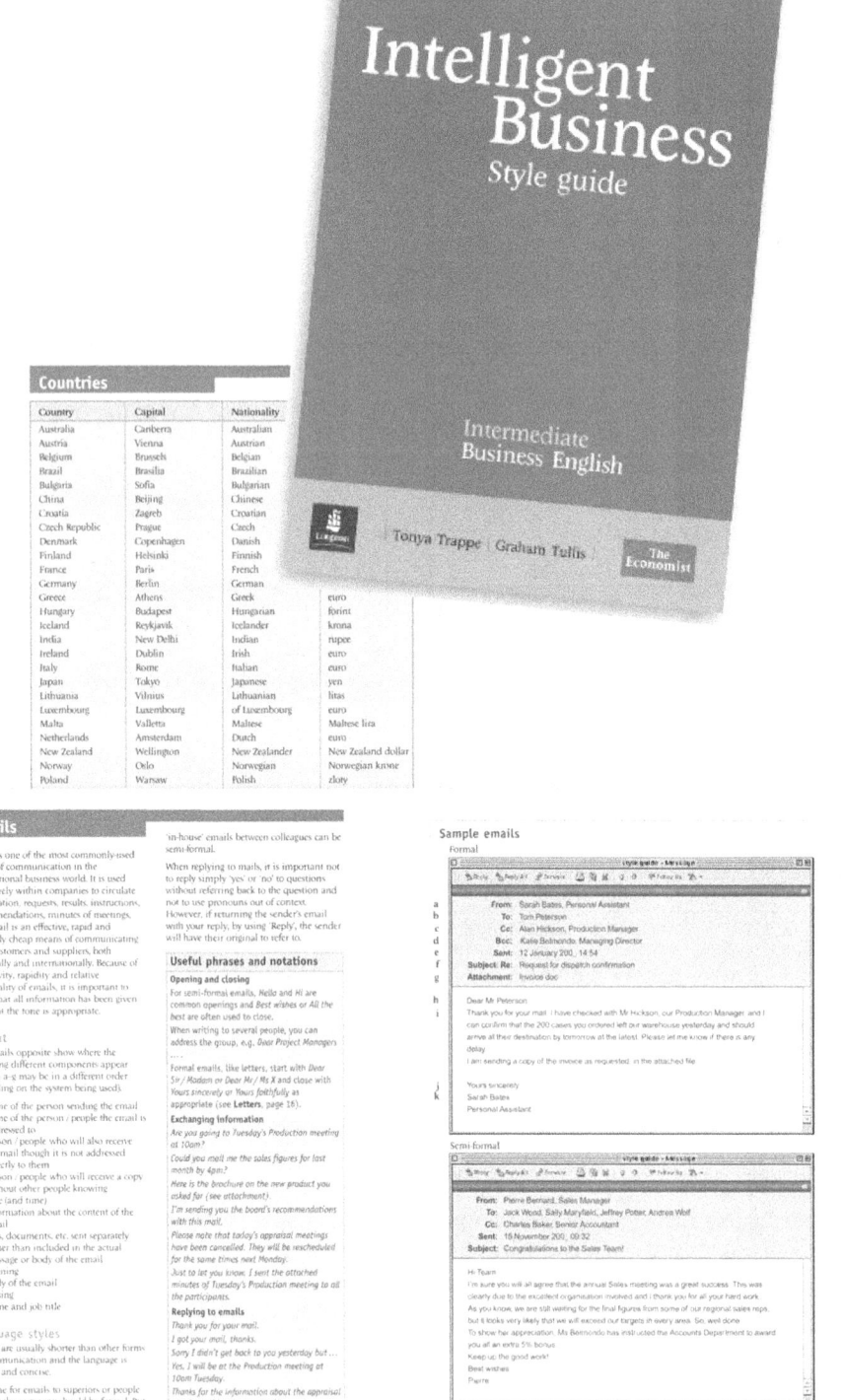

The Workbook consolidates the language of the Coursebook by providing further practice of the key grammar, vocabulary and skills found in the core *Intelligent Business Intermediate* syllabus. Throughout the Workbook there are Cambridge BEC Vantage style tasks to familiarise students with the exam should they wish to take it. At the back of the Workbook is a complete BEC Vantage Practice Test. Finally, the Workbook includes an audio CD containing all the Workbook listening material.

Do Business

Do Business refers to the components developed especially for busy employees who are on a company English language training programme. These components include the *Intelligent Business Intermediate Skills Book* and *Video*. The Skills Book is a self-contained intensive Business English programme providing 30 hours of classroom-based material divided into five days of training. The course is aimed at small groups and built on a syllabus of key business skills such as presenting, socialising and taking part in meetings. The language development work focuses on the functions and communicative strategies required to perform these skills effectively. Unlike in the Coursebook, target language is presented mostly through dialogues and other listening extracts. Students then perform similar tasks and are invited to analyse their own performance. The Skills Book follows the same core syllabus as the Coursebook so the same grammar and functions appear in the equivalent units of both books.

The Skills Book has regular writing sections, a grammar reference with activities, and a *Good Business Practice* reference. The *Culture at Work* syllabus of the Coursebook is followed and expanded upon to explain in detail how national culture can affect international business communication. There is also an interactive CDROM with the Skills Book that contains extra language practice, all the listening material for the book and extracts from the *Intelligent Business Intermediate Video* along with activities. There is also an extensive reference section for grammar, Good Business Practice and Culture at Work.

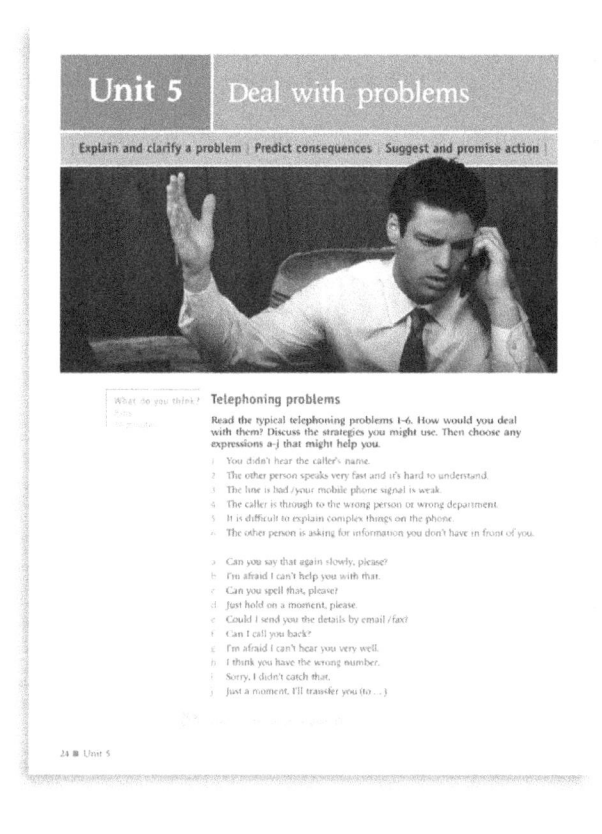

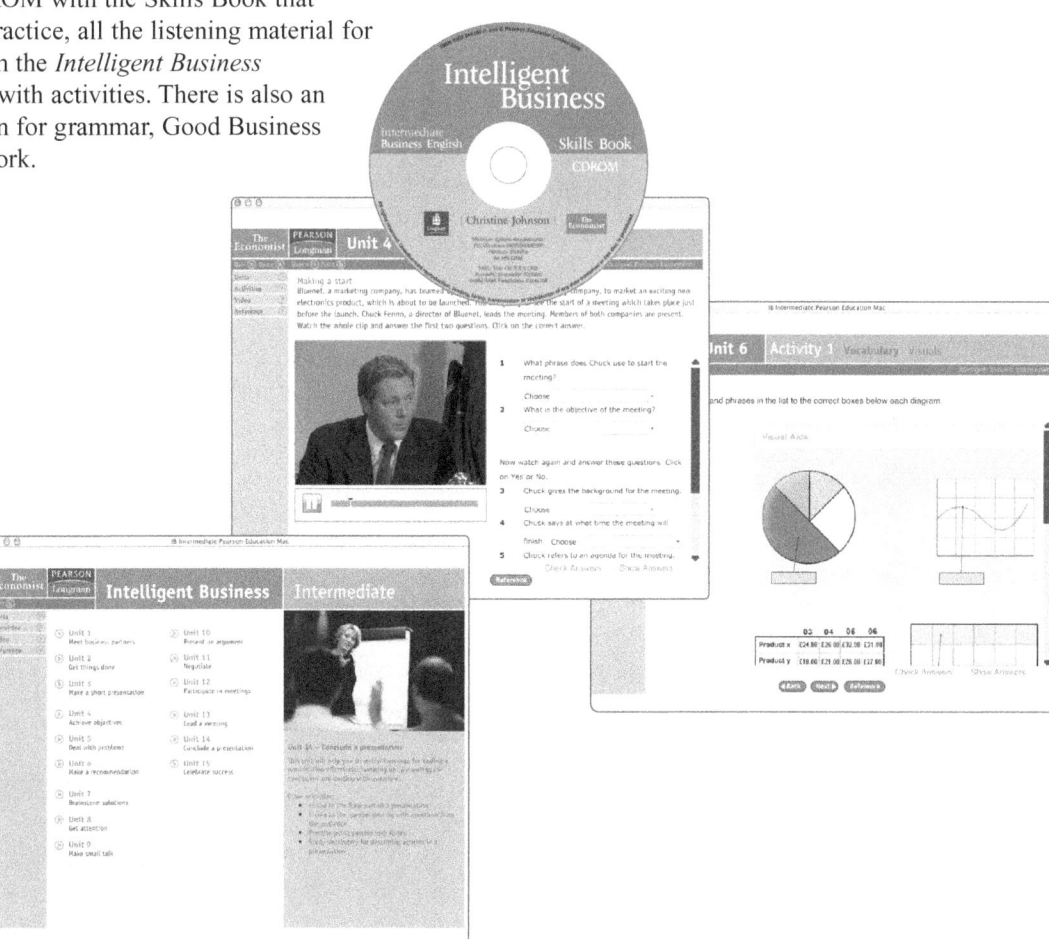

The *Intelligent Business Intermediate Video* is a fictional drama divided into five parts that closely follows the syllabus of the Coursebook. The video illustrates the key business skills from the Skills Book and shows the effect of both national and corporate culture on a partnership between two very different companies.

General support

The key Learn Business and Do Business components are supported by the *Intelligent Business Intermediate Teacher's Book* covering both Coursebook and Skills Book and the *intelligent.business.org* website.

This Teacher's Book is split into two sections: the first covering the Coursebook and Workbook; and the second covering the Skills Book and video. Both sections provide step-by-step notes, answer key and background information, and at the end of each section there is a bank of photocopiable activities.

The *Intelligent Business* website is an entirely free supplement that provides resources for both learners and teachers. For learners there are review questions for each unit of the Coursebook, with which students can interactively measure their progress unit by unit. There is also the premium content that allows access to two free articles from the economist.com subscription website. These articles are updated monthly. For teachers there are handy notes on ideas for making the most of authentic texts. The recipe style notes use Economist texts to demonstrate useful teaching tips on how to exploit the premium content and similar articles from the press.

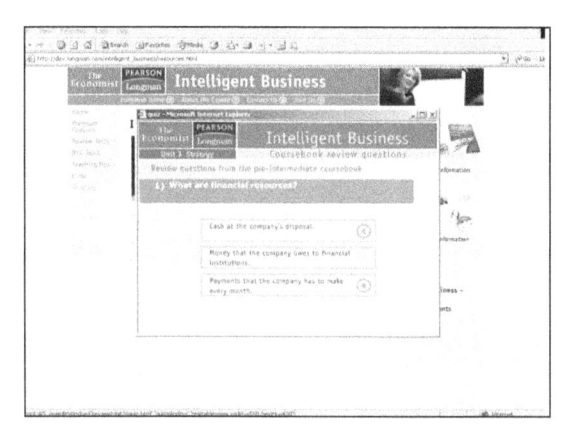

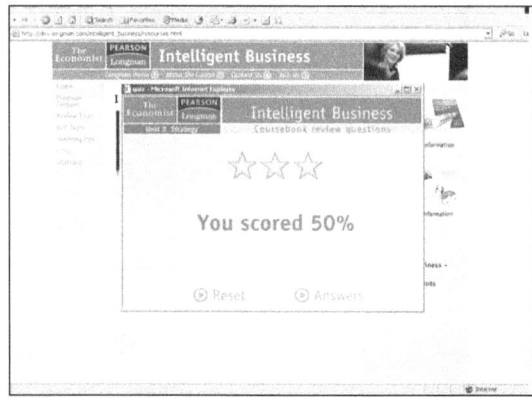

The language of Intelligent Business

All intermediate components of Intelligent Business are based on the same core syllabus. The syllabus is broken down into 15 units and covers four main strands: grammar, vocabulary, functional language and cultural awareness. Although the different components emphasise different strands, they recycle and reaffirm all four key syllabus strands. Furthermore, the different components focus on different language skills in order to present the core syllabus. The Coursebook, for example, focuses on reading skills by introducing key grammar and vocabulary through authentic text, whereas the Skills Book and video focus on listening skills by introducing functional language through transactional dialogues and meetings. The key productive skills of speaking and writing are covered extensively in both the Coursebook and Skills Book.

1 Grammar

The grammar content of the core syllabus is benchmarked against ALTE level 3, Common European Framework level B2 and Cambridge BEC Vantage. The syllabus balances the need for grammatical accuracy required to pass exams with the need for the functional language required to develop fluency and communicative competence quickly.

Each unit of the core syllabus focuses on one grammatical structure. In grammar presentations examples of the target structure are drawn from the previous reading or listening text. The grammar is then highlighted and reviewed. It is assumed that very few students will be seeing the structures for the first time and the approach is very much one of reviewing and consolidating what has been taught before.

The main presentation of grammar is found in the Coursebook. The approach is one of review and students are often asked to demonstrate their knowledge before rules are given. After each grammar presentation there is both written and spoken practice with varying degrees of control, depending on the complexity of the grammar. The Workbook also provides plenty of self-study style grammar practice activities.

There is an extensive Grammar Reference in the back on both the Coursebook and Skills Book and on the Skills Book CDROM. The reference covers all the grammar from the core syllabus and extends the notes provided in the classroom material. As the Skills Book focuses on fluency and communicative effectiveness, there is little explicit grammar presentation within the classroom material. However, this material follows and recycles the core syllabus and the Skills Book CDROM provides a wealth of interactive grammar practice. Furthermore, the grammar reference at the back of the Skills Book also includes integrated practice activities.

2 Vocabulary

In line with the Learn Business, Do Business concept of Intelligent Business, vocabulary is dealt with according to the different needs of the various learners who use the course. For students needing to learn business, the vocabulary focuses on topics that describe the basic structures and functions of the business world. These include company structures, sales, marketing, HR, logistics, pay etc. There are also topics relating to specific issues affecting today's business world such as globalisation and environmental sustainability. Key vocabulary and concepts are introduced in the keynotes, defined, used in context and tested throughout the units. Students are encouraged to activate the vocabulary through speaking and writing activities such as the Dilemma & Decision problem-solving tasks that end each unit. Furthermore, these key items are listed in the Coursebook glossary along with definitions, collocations, synonyms and alternative British and American English usage. There is also an end of glossary vocabulary test. The Workbook provides further extensive recycling and consolidation of the key vocabulary covered in the Coursebook.

For students needing to do business in English, the vocabulary focuses more on functional frameworks rather than individual topic-based items. The Skills Book What do you say? feature reviews communicative strategies and models effective examples through dialogues, presentations and meetings. These key phrases and frameworks are practised interactively on the CDROM and throughout the Skills Book classroom material.

INTELLIGENT BUSINESS (INTERMEDIATE) TEACHER'S BOOK

3 Functional language

As with the vocabulary, the functional language of the core syllabus is dealt with according to whether students need to learn or do business. For students with little experience of hard business skills such as presenting, negotiating and taking part in meetings, the Coursebook presents functional language through the Career Skills feature. Here the language is given general relevance to anyone within an organisation, be it an academic institution or commercial company. These functions include making a case, showing cause and effect and summarising, for example. As with the grammar, items are modelled in context, highlighted and then practised. Further practice can be found in the Workbook.

For students familiar with hard business skills, the functional language is presented in the context of traditional business skills such as negotiating and presenting. Each Career Skill from the Coursebook is transferred to the Skills Book as one of three business subskills in each unit and given a more overtly in-work treatment. Making and responding to offers, for example, becomes Negotiate a win-win solution. The basic functional language is drawn from the core syllabus in both cases but extended and practised more extensively in the Skills Book. As the functional language is so vital for achieving fluency and effective communicative competence, it is the key syllabus strand for the Skills Book and practised extensively throughout. The CDROM provides further interactive support and the Good Business Reference at the back of the Skills Book and on the CDROM provides further guidance on communicative strategies.

4 Cultural awareness

It is now widely accepted that simply learning a common language is no longer enough to prepare people to do business in the global market place. Equally as important as linguistic competence is the ability to understand and deal with the cultural differences that prevent mutually beneficial and rewarding long-term business relationships forming across international borders. Therefore, the final strand of the core Intelligent Business syllabus is cultural awareness.

In each unit a cultural aspect is explored and opposing attitudes are presented. Once more, the content is dealt with according to students' needs and world knowledge. For students learning about business, each cultural aspect is briefly glossed as part of the Career Skills feature in the Coursebook. Without naming nationalities, the opposing behaviours are briefly described and students are asked to consider which attitudes are more familiar to them. They are also invited to discuss how opposing attitudes could cause confusion and possibly conflict between people from different cultures.

For students with knowledge of the working world and experience of cultural differences, the Skills Book presents the same cultural aspect as the Coursebook but explores it in far more detail. The same two opposing ends of the spectrum are considered but the differences in values, attitudes and outward behaviour are discussed in greater depth. As students consider each cultural aspect, they are encouraged to plot their own culture on a Culture profile in the Good Business Reference at the back of the Skills Book. While working through the book this will create a culture curve plotting the values and behaviour of the students' native culture. In multicultural classes the convergence and divergence of the various curves can provide further discussion and comparison. The culture reference notes are also on the CDROM at the back of the Skills Book.

Using Intelligent Business

As all components are built on the core 15-unit intermediate syllabus, the components can be used in various combinations that will consistently cover the same core grammar, skills and cultural issues at the same time. The following combinations are suggestions only and teachers may well wish to mix the various components differently or even all together.

1 Extensive use

Extensive courses delivered over a period of several weeks or even months are usually found in either tertiary institutes or weekly in-service programmes. Such courses can require over 100 hours of material and usually have linguistic knowledge as their goal – in the form of structures and vocabulary. The duration of these courses means that students require substantial practice and regular revision to consolidate what has already been processed. A typical Intelligent Business learning package for such students would include the Coursebook, Workbook and Video. The Coursebook provides a large amount of language input, formal processing of grammar and plenty of written and spoken language practice. There are also reviews every three units. All key vocabulary items that students have to process in order to work through the Coursebook are collected in the unit-for-unit glossary at the back of the Coursebook. Each item includes synonyms and common collocations to help the student activate use of vocabulary. There is also a separate Glossary Test at the end of the section to provide another tool for assessing students' assimilation of the core language of the course.

The Workbook provides further practice of the grammar, vocabulary and functional language presented in the equivalent Coursebook units. It also provides further skills work with many more Economist texts and listening exercises. There are BEC-style tasks to prepare students either for the actual Cambridge exam or for the Practice Test at the back of the Workbook. As the Practice Test recycles many of the themes and vocabulary introduced in the Coursebook, it can be used as an end-of-course assessment. The Workbook is designed as a self-study component with its own key at the back and audio CD inside the back cover.

The Intelligent Business Intermediate video can also be used in conjunction with the Coursebook to demonstrate the Career Skills language used within a corporate environment.

INTELLIGENT BUSINESS (INTERMEDIATE) TEACHER'S BOOK

Alternatively, if the language programme provides enough hours of classroom tuition, the Coursebook and Skills Book can be used together. As they are based on the same core syllabus and share the same 15-unit structure, the Skills Book can be used either immediately after the whole of the Coursebook or integrated on a unit-by-unit basis. The Workbook and Skills Book CDROM will both provide further practice and self-study.

Intelligent Business Intermediate

	Unit 8	Language	Vocabulary	Skills	Culture
Learn Business	Coursebook The bottom line	adjectives and adverbs	corporate governance	referring to visuals	formal and informal presentations
	Workbook Finance	adjectives and adverbs	finance	referring to visuals	
Do Business	Skills Book Get attention, keep attention	adjectives and adverbs	adjectives and adverbs	open a presentation speak with emphasis refer to visuals	formal and informal presentations
	Video	adjectives and adverbs		a presentation referring to visuals	formal and informal presentations

2 Intensive use

As already mentioned, the trend in the corporate Business English sector is for increasingly intensive tuition – but with even more pressure on measurable achievement. Typically, intensive courses are a week long and delivered to small groups or even individual managers. However, even shorter courses of 2-3 days and less are becoming more common. Many schools also provide hybrid courses where an extensive programme delivered over a period of months can have an intensive component built in where students will have a full-day of intensive tuition every so many weeks of extensive study.

The Intelligent Business Skills Book follows the same core 15-unit syllabus as the other components but groups them into 5 blocks of three lessons each – making it perfectly compatible with a standard 5-day intensive programme. The Writing units at the end of each block provide self-study consolidation as does the CDROM (with plenty of practice activities, listening practice and video). The CDROM also provides an option for programming in a self-access centre component to the course. The material is aimed at small groups of up to four students but can be used individually.

The natural support for the Skills Book on an intensive course is the Intelligent Business Intermediate Video. The drama is in five parts, each covering three units of the Skills Book syllabus (i.e. one day on a 5-day course) and closely follows the business skills syllabus, showing these skills in action. The plot of the video involves two very different companies in terms of size, structure and nationality, which provides plenty of discussion points concerning differences in national and corporate culture – as described in the Culture at Work section of the core Intelligent Business Intermediate syllabus.

12

INTRODUCTION

As the Skills Book is very much driven by speaking activities and performance of familiar business tasks, it is essential that students receive feedback on how well they complete these tasks in English. At the end of each unit students are asked to assess their own performance in very general terms and encouraged to discuss what difficulties they experienced. The Teacher's Book also provides frameworks for assessing task performance. The teacher can use these to identify weaknesses and direct students to appropriate materials for further practice.

At the back of the Skills Book and on the CDROM there is an extensive grammar reference with practice activities (for students whose grammar is impeding their ability to complete the tasks successfully). The CDROM also includes many practice activities that target functional language – as well as video clips to demonstrate these functions in use.

3 Exam preparation

Although the Intelligent Business Intermediate Coursebook is not an exam-specific preparation text, it has been developed to meet the criteria for length and difficulty of text applied to Cambridge BEC Vantage exam papers. There are also certain tasks that are similar to typical exam questions. The Coursebook will not prepare students in terms of exam awareness but it will give them an effective command of Business English at intermediate / BEC Vantage level.

For students wishing to take an internationally recognised Business English exam at the end of their course, the Intelligent Business Intermediate Workbook and intelligent.business.org website provide a variety of exam-specific material. The Workbook in particular provides plenty of practice material specifically targeted at the Cambridge BEC Vantage exam. Each Workbook unit contains at least two BEC-style exercises and there is a complete and authentic Practice Test at the back of the book. The Listening Test is included on the audio CD.

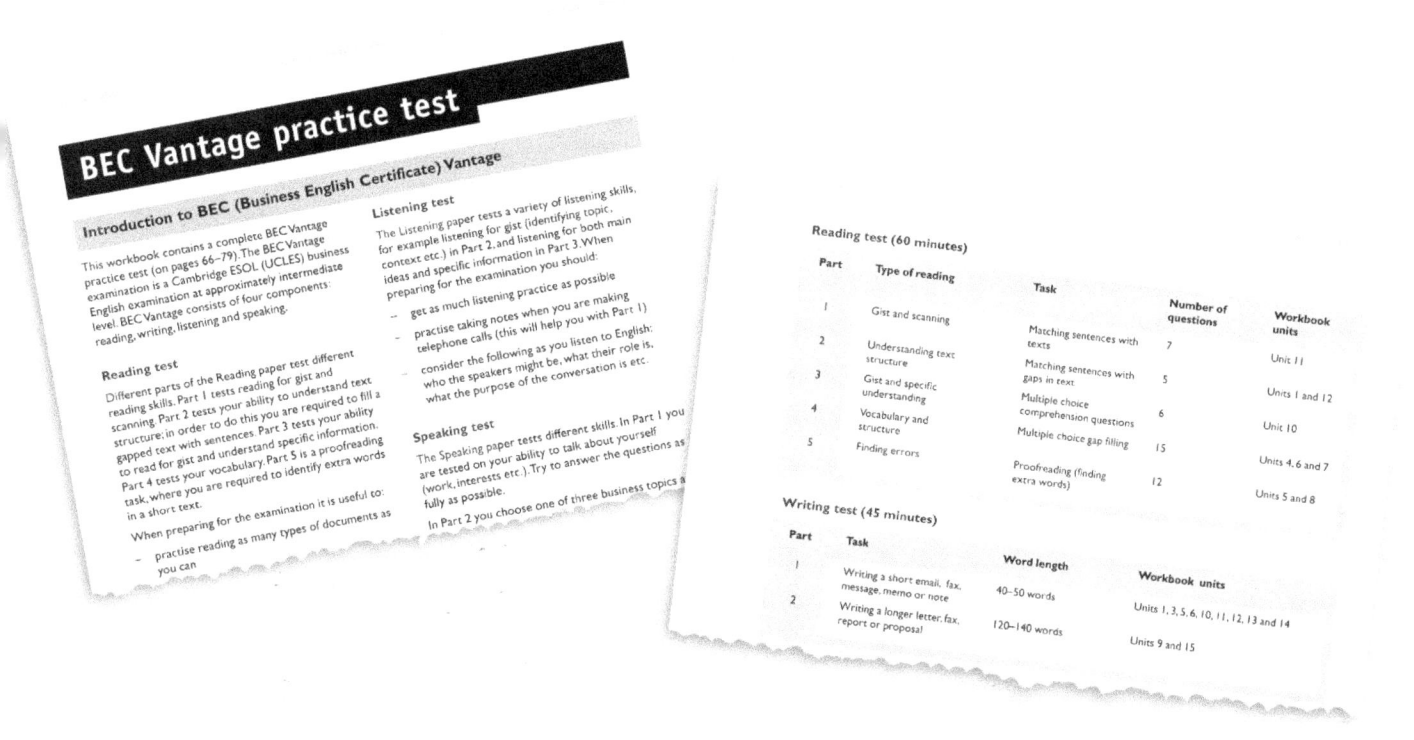

INTELLIGENT BUSINESS (INTERMEDIATE) TEACHER'S BOOK

The intelligent.business.org website provides further BEC exam practice material.

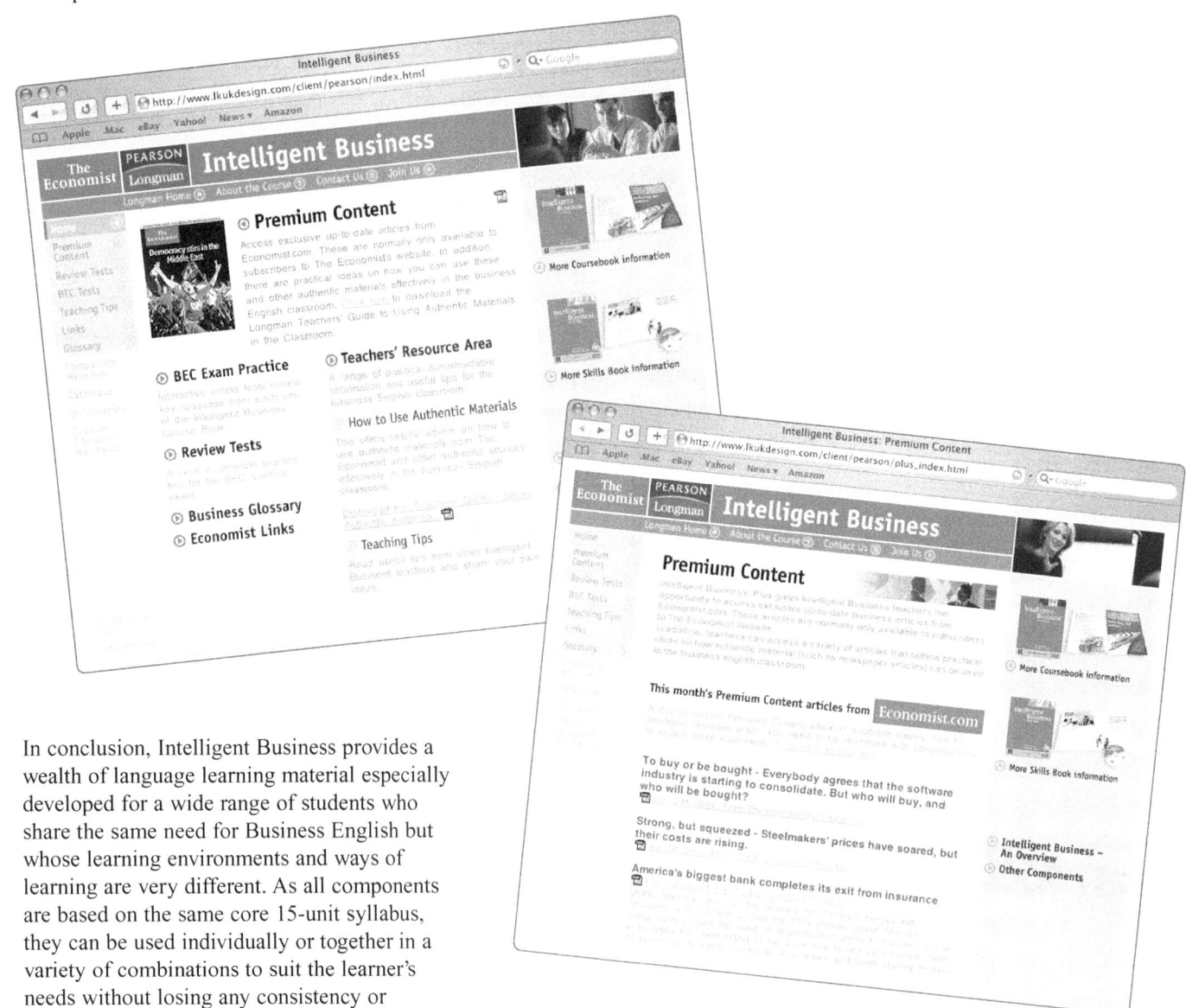

In conclusion, Intelligent Business provides a wealth of language learning material especially developed for a wide range of students who share the same need for Business English but whose learning environments and ways of learning are very different. As all components are based on the same core 15-unit syllabus, they can be used individually or together in a variety of combinations to suit the learner's needs without losing any consistency or continuity of language progression.

Unit 1: Meet business partners

UNIT OBJECTIVES	
Skills:	Introduce yourself
	Talk about your job
	Meet a new business partner
Language:	Present simple and continuous
Culture at work:	Hierarchy

Meeting new business partners may include the following:
- Greetings and introductions
- Making small talk (flight / journey / hotel / weather etc.)
- Making small talk about jobs or the company
- Hospitality (offering a seat / drink etc.)
- Keeping the conversation going (expressing interest / asking follow-up questions etc.)
- Building a positive relationship
- Cultural issues (both national culture and company culture).

Start the lesson by eliciting areas such as those above. Cultural attitudes may affect the language and behaviour that is appropriate in each of these areas. Some language-related cultural considerations when meeting new business partners are:
- Use of first names and / or titles (This may relate to the other person's position in the hierarchy in relation to one's own – but may also vary from culture to culture)
- Order of introductions (e.g. in Japan, a senior member of staff would expect to be introduced before a younger / less senior employee)
- Gestures and body language (Conventions regarding handshaking and the exchanging of business cards may differ from country to country)
- Formality of language (This will vary according to culture and situation).

Task 1

Introduce the topic of the lesson: meeting new business partners. Ask Ss to walk around the room greeting the other Ss, introducing themselves, and asking and answering questions about their companies / jobs. If it is difficult for Ss to walk around the room, ask them simply to turn round in their seats and speak to the nearest Ss. If Ss all work for the same company, ask them to ask and answer questions about their different departments. Note down examples of effectiveness / good uses of language and also mistakes / areas of difficulty. Afterwards, ask Ss if they found out anything unexpected and get some initial feedback as to how effective Ss think they were. Give your feedback. Then use the discussion to link into the next exercise.

What do you say?

Ss match the expressions for greetings and introductions and compare their answers in pairs. Check Ss' answers and elicit more expressions to match the functions. (See Language focus below.) Check Ss are comfortable with the pronunciation of the phrases. If there is time, get Ss to perform mini role-plays using the expressions.

1 g   2 c   3 e   4 h   5 a   6 b   7 f   8 d

Other possible expressions to match the functions
1 How do you do? Nice to meet you.
2 Could you repeat your name?
3 Hello. How are things?
4 It's good to meet you in person after all this time.
5 It's been a long time, hasn't it?
6 My name's Gary Brant. I'm a project manager.
7 This is Julia. She works in production.
8 I don't think we've met.

Optional activity

Develop Ss' awareness of the formality / informality of the expressions for greetings and introductions. Tell Ss that most of the expressions used here are neutral or slightly informal. Can Ss identify any expressions which are more formal? (*How do you do? Pleased to meet you.*) Can Ss identify any words or phrases which are informal? (*Nice to meet you*).

Language focus: Greetings and introductions

The correct response to *How do you do?* is also *How do you do?* This expression is rather formal.

We often respond to greetings by using the same words and adding *too*.
Good to see you.   *Good to see you **too**.*

Sometimes we use alternative words to say the same thing.
Pleased *to meet you.*   ***Good*** *to meet you **too**.*

Task 2

Before Ss do Task 2, elicit possible questions and answers when talking to a new business partner about their company / job. Check Ss can correctly use expressions such as *I'm in charge of ... / My job involves ...* (see Language focus below) and that they are confident about the use of the present simple and continuous to talk about facts / regular events and current activities / temporary situations. In pairs Ss ask one another the questions about their company / job. Then ask Ss to report back on their partner. Monitor Ss' use of present tenses and do additional work on present tenses if necessary.

> **Optional activity**
> **Photocopiable resource 1.1 (page 176)**
> Ss with no work experience may find the task difficult and might find it easier to play a role. If so, prepare the role cards and give a card to each S.

> **Language focus: Talking about your job**
>
> Note the use of noun / -ing following prepositions and certain verbs:
>
> *I'm in charge **of quality assurance**.*
> *I'm responsible **for ensuring** quality.*
> *My job **involves ensuring** that we meet quality standards.*

> **Optional activity**
> **Photocopiable resource 1.2 (page 177)**
> If Ss need further help regarding the use of present tenses, do a card sorting exercise. The photocopiable resource consists of Set 1 (a set of header cards with example sentences) and Set 2 (a set of header cards with non-continuous verbs). Prepare both sets of cards for each pair. First, focus on the basic uses of the present simple and continuous. Elicit the uses of the two present forms. Then give a Set 1 to each pair. Ask Ss to identify the header cards then group the remaining cards under the appropriate headings. Clarify any misunderstandings and get Ss to think of further example sentences for each use.
>
> **Answers (Set 1)**
> **Regular events:** How often do you visit your clients? We meet every Tuesday. They don't usually reply to emails straight away.
> **Facts:** Who does she report to? I don't work in a team. My company provides financial advice to clients.
> **Events happening now:** Are you enjoying this seminar? We're working on a project to improve customer relations. They're not attending this meeting.
> **Temporary situations:** He's not travelling so much while his health's not good. Are you offering discounts this month? I'm working at Head Office this week.
>
> Then elicit the fact that some verbs are not usually used in the continuous form. Elicit the categories used on the header cards. Give a Set 2 to each pair and get Ss to do a similar sorting exercise. Once again, elicit example sentences.
>
> **Answers (Set 2)**
> **Verbs of opinion / feeling:** want, think, understand, mean, prefer, like
> **Verbs of the senses:** taste, hear, see, feel, smell
> **Verbs of ownership:** belong, have

Analysis, Task 2

Allow Ss a couple of minutes to reflect on the Analysis questions and discuss them in pairs. Ask Ss to report back and discuss their comments. You may wish to elicit useful phrases for checking understanding (e.g. *I'm sorry, I didn't catch that*).

Skills book, Grammar reference: Present simple and continuous, page 83

> **Hierarchy**
> Hierarchy refers to the distance between different layers of staff and management in an organisation. Recently there has been a trend to restructure, removing levels of management and producing a flatter hierarchy, in order to cut costs and improve communication. Some organisations have also seen moves towards regrouping staff into project teams.

Culture at work

Draw an organigram on the board to introduce the idea of steep and flat hierarchy. Ask Ss which kind of hierarchy is common in their country and to suggest companies they know with each type of hierarchy. Ask Ss to give examples of things that might indicate hierarchy within a company, e.g. office size, parking spot, class of flight ticket, desk space, company car. Then ask Ss to look at the three categories about hierarchy on page 7 and to relate these categories to the companies they mentioned. Also ask Ss to think about their own company in terms of physical indicators of hierarchy and in terms of the three categories. Then ask Ss to complete their own culture profile about hierarchy on page 82. (Ss identify and mark with a cross where they believe their culture is situated on the line ranging from Steep to Flat. You may wish to ask Ss to write two marks on the line: a cross indicating

UNIT 1

their organisational culture, and a circle indicating the culture in general in their country.) Explain that when meeting new business partners, Ss may come across hierarchies different to those in their own company. Which types of hierarchy, in Ss' opinions, generate better communication, more efficient decision-making processes, more promotion opportunities etc? Which type of hierarchy would they prefer to work in? NB: Be diplomatic as some Ss may be offended if it is implied that the hierarchy in which they work is not very effective.

Skills book, Culture profile, page 82

What do you think?

Before starting the activity, ask what kinds of people visit the Ss' company and what Ss do when receiving such visitors. Ss then put the items in the list into a possible order and compare their answers in pairs before discussing them with the whole group. Are there any items Ss would not do? Would they add anything to the list?

Skills book, Good business practice, Socialising, Meeting new business partners, page 80

Listening 1

Before playing the CD, explain that Ss are going to hear Paul Larousse visiting Lisa Guzman at head office. As they listen, Ss number the items in the list from the previous activity in the order Lisa does them. Play the listening as many times as necessary.

> 1 Greet the visitor with a formal greeting / Say good morning or good afternoon
> 2 Introduce yourself
> 3 Ask about their journey to your company
> 4 Invite your visitor to sit down
> 5 Offer something to drink
> 6 Ask about your visitor's company and work

Listening 2

Play the listening again, several times if necessary, for Ss to pick out the expressions Lisa used. Then refer Ss to the audioscript on page 105. Ensure Ss are happy with the pronunciation of the phrases.

> **Apologising:** Sorry to keep you waiting.
> **Asking about Paul's journey:** How was your trip? How long does it take from Canada?
> **Inviting Paul to sit down:** Please – have a seat.
> **Offering something to drink:** Would you like a cup of coffee – or tea?

Task 3

Check Ss understand each situation. Allow Ss time to prepare their roles in pairs and remind them of some key language. Monitor the pairs as they work through the situations.

Analysis, Task 3

Allow Ss time to reflect on the questions individually, then start a group discussion. Give your feedback on the Ss' performance. Refer both to effective language and any gaps / difficulties. Teach additional useful polite phrases that can be used when meeting a business partner, e.g. *I'm looking forward to working with you.*

Self-assessment

Allow Ss a few minutes to think about what they have achieved from the unit and tick the boxes. Suggest what Ss can do to gain further practice.

Video, Part 1

CD-Rom

INTELLIGENT BUSINESS (INTERMEDIATE) TEACHER'S BOOK: SKILLS BOOK

Unit 2: Get things done

UNIT OBJECTIVES

Skills:	Talk about urgency
	Persuade people to do things
	Get things done on time
Language:	Modal verbs (*can, could, would, may, might*)
	Time phrases
Culture at work:	Being direct

It is usually important to do the following when trying to get things done:
- Define the task clearly
- Decide success criteria
- Be clear of the time-frame you are working to
- Know what resources are available (people, budget, knowledge etc.)
- Know how this task fits into the overall picture (Is the task important / urgent?).

Some tasks may be urgent, but not important. Some may be both important and urgent. Prioritising tasks can be difficult due to external pressures (e.g. pressure from clients).

Cultural attitudes in the following areas may affect how people get things done:
- Attitudes to time (Some cultures consider timescales to be very important and adhere to them at all costs, e.g. working long hours. Other cultures have a more casual attitude and consider work will be done when it can; other aspects of life, e.g. family life and holidays, play as important a role as work)
- Attitudes to uncertainty (Some cultures plan schedules rigorously to ensure that schedules are under control. Other cultures feel less need to plan in such detail)
- Levels of directness (See below).

What do you think?

Introduce the topic of the lesson: getting things done on time. Ask Ss the sorts of things they do to help them keep to deadlines and how they decide which tasks have the greatest priority. Write any key vocabulary on the board including different word forms, e.g. *priority / prioritise* and *urgent / urgency*. Then refer Ss to the list and ask them to tick the things they do. Collect responses, developing the discussion if time, e.g. how do they estimate the time needed for each task?

Skills book, Good business practice, Meetings, Getting things done on time, page 79

What do you say?

Elicit from Ss what they could say to stress that something is urgent (e.g. *the deadline is today, we need it as soon as possible / by the end of today*). Then ask Ss to order the sentences from most urgent (1) to least urgent (5). Check Ss' answers. Draw Ss' attention to the time phrases *before*, *by* and *as soon as possible*. Explain that you will return to these later.

1 b 2 d 3 c 4 a 5 e

Listening 1

Ss now listen to someone trying to get something done: a sales manager organising a golf tournament. Check Ss understand the list of actions to be done and the plan. As Ss listen, they write the actions (a–g) into the plan. If Ss find this difficult, tell them simply to order the actions then copy the letters into the plan afterwards. Ss compare answers in pairs before you check the answers together.

1 e 2 c 3 b 4 g 5 a 6 f 7 d

Listening 2

Ss listen again, looking at the audioscript on page 105, and pick out language for talking about when things must be done. Move on to a review of the use of *by* and time phrases (*before, after, until* etc.) in time clauses with the present tense (see Language focus on the next page).

We want to fix it for the 10th of April – so we don't have much time.
This is urgent so we must do it right away.
We need to book as soon as possible.
We won't know exactly until we invite the customers.
By the end of February.
I'll tell the salespeople to send out the invitations as soon as we know the hotel.
We want to have coffee when the guests arrive.
Before we choose the menu for lunch we need to check.
I'd appreciate it if you could let me know the special requirements by the third week of March.
I'd like to get everything done before April if possible.
There's no rush – we can do that any time.

124

UNIT 2

Language focus: Time clauses (with *by*, *when*, *before*, *until* etc.)

We use *by* to talk about deadlines.
*It's important to get confirmation **by** the end of February.*

When we use a verb to talk about future deadlines, we usually use *by the time* + present simple.
*We'll need everything agreed **by the time** we **meet**.*

We use the present tense (usually present simple) to refer to future time after the following words: *when, as soon as, before, after, until*.
*I'll tell the salespeople to send out the invitations **as soon** as we **know** the hotel.*
*We want to have lunch **when** the guests **arrive**.*
***Before** we **choose** the menu for lunch, we need to check special requirements.*

We can use the present perfect if we want to stress that one action is complete before another starts.
*We'll brief the sales team **when** we'**ve agreed** on all the arrangements.*

Task 1

Ensure Ss understand that Action 3 (inviting the customers) and Action 4 (confirming the number of guests) have not yet been done – so action needs to be taken urgently. Allocate the roles to Ss in pairs (one is the Sales Manager and the other is the Conference Organiser from the listening) for Ss to discuss the action to be taken. Listen and provide feedback, focusing on the target language.

> **Optional activity**
> **Photocopiable resource 2.1 (page 178)**
> This activity provides personalised practice in the use of time clauses using the correct tense. Give out a planning sheet to each S and a time limit. Ss think of a task and note it with the deadline in the band at the top. They then quickly note below five steps that need to be taken in order to meet this deadline. (If Ss simply list the steps chronologically, no complex language will be needed.) Ss then exchange their information without showing the planning sheet. They should use time phrases, e.g. *by, when, as soon as, before, after, until* to clarify the order in which things need to be done. (If they forget information, they can add it afterwards, e.g. *Before we do that, we've got to collect all the data.*) Encourage Ss to ask each other questions if anything is not clear. Monitor and give feedback on the language including the use of tenses.

Task 2

Ss are going to persuade others to help them meet their deadlines. Before Ss look at the language listed, write the request *Can you help me* on the board and elicit from Ss how this can be made more polite or more tentative (i.e. not taking the speaker's agreement for granted). Then point Ss to the phrases. Remind them that *mind* is followed by *–ing* and *I'd appreciate …* is followed by *it*. Also refer Ss to the Grammar reference section on requests on page 87, drawing attention to typical responses (e.g. *That could be rather difficult*). Check pronunciation. When Ss are confident with the language of requests and persuasion, divide Ss into groups of four and distribute roles A–D on pages 98, 100, 102 and 104. Ideally Ss should not see the other roles. Remind Ss to try to use appropriate language for persuading and responding. Set a time limit. Listen and make notes for later feedback.

Skills book, Grammar reference: Modal verbs, part 1, page 87

> **Optional activity**
> Before giving Ss the roles for Task 2, do some controlled practice of language for requests. Elicit six phrases for making a request ranging from direct and not particularly polite (1) to most indirect / polite (6). Write these in a column on the left-hand side of the board in the correct order from 1 to 6. Then elicit six requests (e.g. open the window, attend a meeting instead of me, work overtime, lend me a CD). Write these in a column on the right-hand side of the board. Now ask Ss to work in pairs and give a dice to each pair. Ss take turns to make and respond to requests, working down the list on the right. The language they use is determined by the roll of the dice, e.g. depending on the phrases Ss have suggested, Phrase 6 could be *I'd really appreciate it if you could* open the window. Ss then decide if they can think of a situation when this language would be appropriate. If they think it would not be appropriate, they modify the language. (In this case, the request may be too polite and tentative for the situation; *Could you open the window?* would be more appropriate.)

Analysis, Task 2

Allow Ss a few minutes to reflect on their performance of Task 2. Ss then report back on how effectively they persuaded their colleagues to help and the language they used to do this. Add feedback from your own notes.

> **Levels of directness**
>
> Indirectness is considered polite in British culture but may not be in other cultures. Cultural differences in levels of directness can cause difficulties as attitudes can be very deeply rooted. For example, a British person working in a shop may be offended by a non-native speaker saying *Give me a newspaper*; on the other hand, the standard British request *Could you give me a newspaper?* may sound ridiculous translated into Portuguese in Brazil. Differences in levels of directness can lead to frustration as well as causing offence. Therefore, when using English as an international language, it is important to bear in mind the culture of the person you are working with and the expectations they might have in terms of levels of directness. The language used to make a request may vary according to three factors:
>
> - culture, e.g. Saudi and Dutch people communicating with different levels of directness
> - relationship, e.g. boss to subordinate
> - situation, e.g. asking someone to do something beyond their normal job.

Culture at work

Before Ss look at the table, ask them about their views on directness:

- *In your culture, is there a tendency to be direct or indirect?*
- *Can you think of any other cultures which are similar in this respect?*
- *Can you think of any cultures which are very different from yours in this respect?*
- *Give examples of experiences when you have noticed this difference.*
- *How did these experiences make you feel?*
- *Do you prefer to be direct or indirect?*

Then asks Ss to look at the table about being direct. Elicit further examples of direct / indirect language in English. Ensure that Ss realise that the language used to make a request is not only dependent upon culture (see Levels of directness above). Then ask Ss to complete their own culture profile about being direct on page 82. (Ss identify and mark with a cross where they believe their culture is situated on the line ranging from Direct to Indirect.)

Skills book, Culture profile, page 82

Task 3

Explain Ss are going to hold a short meeting to plan what is to be done when and by whom. Ss read through the task and the information about the three projects. Focus on the first project together as an example and encourage Ss to suggest answers to the questions in ovals. Only when they have thought about these questions can they start to plan the project. Divide the group into groups of 3–4. Point out the time limit, and that a different person should lead the discussion of each project. Remind Ss to try and activate some of the language they have been learning about getting things done. They should make notes in the table provided on page 101. Monitor the activity and take notes for use during feedback.

Analysis, Task 3

Allow Ss a little time to reflect, then ask for comments. Ss should focus on effectiveness. Then provide your own additional language feedback related to their points.

Self-assessment

Allow Ss a few minutes to think about what they have achieved from the unit and tick the boxes. Suggest what Ss can do to gain further practice.

Video, Part 1

CD-Rom

Unit 3: Make a short presentation

UNIT OBJECTIVES	
Skills:	Prepare a short introduction
	Sequence points and make a summary
	Give a short presentation
Language:	Future forms
Culture at work:	Attitudes to time

This unit provides an introduction to making presentations. This skill is further developed in Units 6, 8 and 14. (It is also developed in Units 3, 8 and 14 of the Coursebook.) The following may be important when making a short presentation:
- Preparation (to ensure you have something to say and that you say it well)
- Clear structure
- Signposting (to help your listeners follow you)
- Clear pronunciation
- Interest (interesting content and interesting delivery, including the use of stress and pauses)
- Eye contact with the audience
- Appropriate body language
- Visual support for the listeners.

Cultural attitudes may affect the language and behaviour that is appropriate when giving your presentation:
- Timing and structure (Some cultures may keep to exact timing whereas others may be comfortable with looser structuring. See Culture at work)
- Eye contact (It may be embarrassing if you make direct eye contact with individuals. Instead, it may be more appropriate to look across the room without focusing on any individual)
- Gestures and body language (Some cultures use the body to support verbal communication more than other cultures)
- Formality of language (This will vary according to culture and situation)
- Use of jokes and humour (This will vary according to culture and situation: in some cultures using a joke is considered positive; in other cultures it is inappropriate).

What do you think?

Introduce the topic of the lesson: making short presentations. Elicit possible topics of presentations and what Ss think makes an effective presentation. Refer Ss to the list on page 14. Ask Ss to tick those items they think are essential to include and discuss them. You may wish to expand on cultural differences relating to the use of jokes.

Skills book, Good business practice, Presentations, Making an effective presentation, page 76

What do you say?

Elicit why the structure of a presentation is important. Point Ss to a possible structure as shown in the flow diagram on page 15. Ss match a phrase with each step. Check Ss' answers. Check Ss are comfortable with the pronunciation of the phrases, particularly sentence stress.

1 e   2 c   3 f   4 b   5 a   6 g   7 d

Task 1

Explain Ss are going to do a task involving the introduction to a presentation. Ensure Ss understand the situation with Leena and AYT.

Step 1: In small groups, Ss consider the questions and prepare the introduction to the presentation.

Step 2: Ss take turns to present to the other members of the group. During the presentations make notes on clarity, use of structuring phrases and future forms. Give feedback. Take this opportunity to review the future forms relevant to a presentation and the use of signposting (see Language focus on the next page).

1 Leena should say something like *My name is Leena Perttonen and I'm the marketing manager at AYT*
2 an overview of AYT
3 to give reasons why the Polish developers should choose AYT for its construction project
4 general information about AYT, AYT's international experience, reasons for AYT's success

Skills book, Grammar reference: Future forms, page 84

INTELLIGENT BUSINESS (INTERMEDIATE) TEACHER'S BOOK: SKILLS BOOK

Language focus: Future forms in presentations

Presenters may choose different future forms in a presentation.
First I'll talk about the background to the problem (spontaneous decision)
First I'm going to talk about the background to the problem (personal intention; the presentation is well planned)

Alternatively, speakers may choose phrases with no future form.
First I'd like to talk about … / First I want to talk about …

The form used is generally a personal choice, rather than a matter of correctness. Typical mistakes (to be avoided) by non-native speakers in presentations are as follows.
~~Now I move on to the reasons for this decision~~ (incorrect use of the present to refer to the future)
~~First I will tell you about the history of the company, then I will talk about the current structure of the company and finally I will move onto our plans for the future~~ (over-use of *will*)

Listening 1 ▮1▮

Explain that Ss are now going to hear Leena's introduction to her presentation. Play Part 1 and ask Ss to listen and note down how Leena's introduction was similar / different to theirs. Ss compare notes with the others in their small group. In feedback, focus on the phrases Leena actually used, drawing attention to the verbs (*outline, point out* etc.). You may wish to ask one S to present the introduction again.

Listening 1 ▮2▮

Ss are now going to listen to the complete presentation. Write the sections of Leena's presentation on the board (**1** *General information,* **2** *International experience* and **3** *Reasons for success*) and ask Ss to take notes under each heading as you play the whole presentation (CD Track 5 contains the complete presentation, i.e. Part 1 and Part 2). Elicit Ss' answers. Then ask Ss to listen again and write down the phrases Leena uses to sequence the points in her presentation. Collate the answers and check pronunciation. Elicit any alternative phrases that Ss could use.

a Section 1 intro: So, let me start with the company.
b Section 1 ending: Well, that was some general information about the company.
c Section 2 intro: Now I'll move on to our international operations.
d Section 3 intro: And so to my final point: the reasons for our success.
e Summing up: So – to sum up.

Language focus: Signposting

A presentation can be made more effective through the use of signposting. Sometimes future forms are used for signposting. Useful phrases include:
So, let me start with… / Right, I'd like to start with… / To start, I want to…
OK, that was … / So, that covers…
Now I'll move onto… / Moving onto… / Now, I'd like to move onto…
And so to my final point, … / Coming now to my last point, …. / That brings me to my final point, …

In addition to signposting, sequencing words can help the audience.
First *I'd like to start by giving you the background.*
Secondly *I'll outline the problem.*
Next *I want to discuss the implications.*
Finally *I'm going to suggest some solutions.*

Task 2

Divide the Ss into pairs. A looks at Presentation A; B looks at Presentation B. Ask Ss to suggest an appropriate order for the points in their presentation. Ss do not need to think of any detailed content.

Step 1: Ss think of and practise phrases for introducing and ending each section, using the information given in Presentation A or B. Ss simply link the points given, using signposting phrases (See Langue focus above), e.g. *I'm going to start with our strategic objectives and plans for future growth … OK, those were our strategic objectives. Now let me move on to the history of our company.*

Step 2: Now ask Ss to think of what they would include in their summary. Ss think of expressions to introduce the summary and link the points before practising in pairs. Ask some Ss to present to the whole group. Give feedback.

UNIT 3

> **Attitudes to time**
> The concept of time can vary widely from culture to culture. For some people, time plays an important role and is watched carefully, e.g. arriving punctually to appointments, starting meetings on time, finishing presentations after the specified amount of time. For others, it is an approximate guideline for business and life – meetings start roughly around the agreed time, lunches run overtime and presentations may last longer than anticipated. Within the context of a presentation, a person's attitude to time can also be shown through the way in which they structure their presentation, how they sequence their thoughts and how they follow the plan.

Culture at work

Ask Ss whether they have ever given a presentation that has run on longer than planned. How did the audience react? Do they think timing is an important aspect of giving a presentation? Do other cultures have the same opinion? Can they give any examples from their experience? Refer Ss to the table on page 17. Where does their culture fit? Then ask Ss to complete their own culture profile about attitudes to time on page 82. (Ss identify and mark with a cross where they believe their culture is situated on the line ranging from Precise timing to Approximate timing. You may wish to ask Ss to write two marks on the line: a cross indicating their organisational culture, and a circle indicating the culture in general in their country.)

Skills book, Culture profile, page 82

Task 3

Step 1: Using the framework (flow chart) provided on page 15, Ss prepare a mini-presentation about their own organisation. Pre-experience Ss may choose to a) talk about their college, b) do a presentation about a famous company that they know, c) work out a profile of an imaginary company as the basis of the presentation. Alternatively, set the preparation as homework, and Ss give the presentation in the next lesson.

Step 2: Ss give their presentations to the whole group (or to sub-groups if the class is large). Listen and take notes on good performance and areas of weakness.

Analysis, Task 3

Allow Ss a few minutes to reflect on the questions individually, then start a group discussion. Give your own feedback. Refer to effective language and any gaps / difficulties.

Self-assessment

Allow Ss a few minutes to think about what they have achieved from the unit and tick the boxes. Suggest what Ss can do to gain further practice.

> **Optional activity**
> You may want to extend the presentation task. If so, consider using the Presentation preparation and feedback frameworks on pages 186 and 187.

Skills book, Units 6, 8 and 14, pages 28, 38 and 66
Coursebook, Units 3, 8 and 14, pages 29, 73 and 125
Teacher's book, pages 29, 60, 96, 138, 146 and 168
Video, Part 1
CD-Rom

INTELLIGENT BUSINESS (INTERMEDIATE) TEACHER'S BOOK: SKILLS BOOK

Writing 1: Informal emails

UNIT OBJECTIVES	
Skills:	Get things done politely
	Sequence the points in your message
Language:	Articles

It is important to consider the following in relation to any type of writing, including emails:
- The reader (What is the relationship to the writer? Does the language need to be formal or informal? How polite does the writer need to be? What is the reader's level of knowledge of the subject and level of English?)
- The purpose (What are you trying to achieve through your writing?)
- The medium (Is sending an email the best medium? Or would a phone call be more effective?)
- Structure (What is the best way to structure the email and sequence the points?)
- Clarity, conciseness and consistency
- Accuracy (grammar, spelling, punctuation).

Cultural attitudes (varying according to national culture and also organisational culture) may have an impact on the following:
- Formality of language
- The extent to which emails share the characteristics of other written correspondence.

Style guide, Emails, page 18

Style guide, General rules, page 3

Style guide, Organising your writing, page 4

Teacher's book, Writing preparation framework, page 188

Teacher's book, Writing feedback framework, page 189

What do you think? page 18 **1**

Introduce the topic. Ask Ss what sort of emails they write, for what purpose and to whom. Do they generally need to be polite in their emails? What if something is urgent or they need help? Then ask Ss to look at the emails and decide which email is more polite. Ensure Ss realise it depends on who they are writing to (the recipient). Ss decide which of the two emails is more polite. Then Ss look at the list of four recipients and answer the questions. Point out that B is more polite according to UK / US writing conventions; notions of politeness may be different in their own culture.

What do you think? page 18 **2**

Ss underline the polite phrases from Email B, then compare with a partner. Point out that writing politely does not just involve particular phrases; Ss need to consider what the reader will think is appropriate.

1 Email B is more polite. Email A could be written to a close colleague; however, Email B might also be written to a colleague in certain circumstances. Email B could be written to the other recipients. (See Language focus below.)

2 I know you're busy but …, Is there any way you can …, I'd really appreciate it

Language focus: Informality and politeness in writing

Sometimes register (i.e. formality / informality) and tone (i.e. politeness / impoliteness) are confused – but they are different things. Email B is informal (*Hi Jean*, contractions, *really*, *Thanks*) but it is polite and the writer does not take the reader for granted; instead, the writer recognises that the reader is busy, makes a polite request and emphasises his thanks.

Email A is written to a close colleague. Therefore, the writer does not bother to write the recipient's name and is very direct. However, as all writing is open to interpretation by the reader, such directness could suggest lack of respect. Therefore, it is important to consider your reader when writing even a simple informal email.

The following phrases move from more direct to less direct:
Can you …?
Could you …?
Is there any way you can …?
Is there any way you could …?
I'd appreciate it if you could …?

Teacher's book, page 126

130

WRITING 1

Task 1

Before Ss start to write, ensure they understand the situation. *Consolidated figures* refer to the combined accounts from all divisions or subsidiaries. Elicit the level of formality needed and the appropriate tone. (You do not know Hella but she works for the same large company so you can be informal. However, you need to be firm but polite.) Ss write the email individually, if possible using a computer and sending the email to a partner. Then encourage peer correction before giving feedback.

> **Suggested answer**
> Dear Hella
> I've just started working as assistant accountant at head office and I need the quarterly figures from all divisions at the end of the month for consolidation purposes. Is there any way you could send me the northeast division's figures by tomorrow? I'd really appreciate it.
> Looking forward to receiving the figures.
> Regards
> *Mona*

> **Optional activity**
> For homework, Ss write Hella's email in response.

What do you think? page 19 1

Ask Ss how many emails they receive each day. How do they decide which ones to read first? Collate ideas on the board. Refer Ss to the list of hints for making an email easier to read. Do they agree?

> There is not a single correct answer. However, one of the most important things is to put important information near the start of the email. It is usually a good idea to keep the message short. If this is impossible, it is a good idea to use headings or to number points so that the reader notices individual sections.

What do you write? 2

Ss match the recommended sequence of points and jumbled message. Check Ss' answers. Do they agree the order is logical? Then ask Ss to organise the email into paragraphs. Elicit any informal elements of the email (contractions, *Thanks*). Then elicit examples of polite language (*I'm afraid I may not be able to, would it be possible to, please let me know if that's a problem for you, please note that, thanks for, I'm looking forward very much to*).

At the top: 1 Hello Ili
Para 1: 2 Thanks for sending the agenda for our meeting
3 I'm afraid I may not be able to …
4 Would it be possible …
Para 2: 5 You asked me to …
Para 3: 6 I'm looking forward …
At the bottom: 7 Best regards, Jacqui

Task 2

Ensure Ss understand the writing task and emphasise the importance of correct sequencing. You may prefer Ss to do the writing task as homework.

> **Suggested answer**
> Dear Jacqui
> Thanks for your message and the feasibility report.
> Yes, we could start the meeting at 9.00, but would it be possible to finish at 16.00 as I have an appointment later? Is there any way we can have a shorter lunch break so we could finish a little earlier?
> Looking forward to seeing you next week.
> Regards

> **Optional activity**
> You may want to extend the writing task. If so, consider using the Writing preparation and feedback frameworks on pages 188 and 189.

> **Optional activity**
> You may want to integrate further practice in writing emails with a review of an area of grammar: articles. Articles are complex and best taught over a number of lessons. Therefore, focus on only one particular area of difficulty regarding articles, such as the incorrect use of *the* with general plural and uncountable nouns when no article should be used (a typical mistake of French Ss, e.g. ~~the~~ *satisfaction with the product is high*). Review this area, referring Ss to the relevant section on page 94. Before the class, write an email including examples of the typical mistake. Give Ss a jumbled version for Ss to reorder the email, correct the use of articles and write an email in response.

Skills book, Grammar reference, Articles, page 94

INTELLIGENT BUSINESS (INTERMEDIATE) TEACHER'S BOOK: SKILLS BOOK

Unit 4: Achieve objectives

UNIT OBJECTIVES	
Skills:	Set objectives
	Open a meeting
	Evaluate performance
Language:	Present perfect and past simple
Culture at work:	Fixed objectives or flexibility?

This unit provides an introduction to taking part in meetings. This skill is further developed in Units 7, 12 and 13. Participating in a meeting may mean different things and involve different roles. Meetings are not always formal with a printed agenda; nor do they always have an official chairperson. However, most meetings do have a leader of some kind. For those students who need to lead a meeting, the following may need to be considered:
- Having a clear agenda and planning what is to be achieved in the time (the objectives)
- Keeping an eye on the time
- Encouraging every participant to contribute
- Dealing with any disagreements
- Aiming to reach a clear decision or plan of action (who is to do what and by when)
- Summarising.

For those students who do not need to lead a meeting but need to be able to participate actively and effectively, the following may need to be considered:
- Being clear about the agenda and what is to be achieved (the objectives)
- Listening actively, checking and clarifying if necessary
- Offering ideas and opinions, giving reasons
- Reacting to the comments made by the other participants.

Cultural attitudes may have an impact on the following meeting-related aspects:
- Following a fixed agenda / objectives or allowing the meeting to evolve
- Spending time on small talk before the meeting or getting straight down to business
- Allowing interruptions during the meeting
- Holding the meeting in a social setting, e.g. the golf course.

What do you think?

Introduce the topic of the lesson: achieving objectives in meetings, with the main focus on opening a meeting and setting the objectives of the meeting. Ask Ss how often they or their colleagues go to meetings, how big the meetings generally are and whether they always have a clear purpose. (Ensure that pre-experience Ss realise they can also answer this question, e.g. with reference to gatherings at college.) Refer Ss to the exercise and the first two bullet points. As a group, brainstorm why people hold meetings and collate a list on the board. Develop any useful verb + noun phrases, e.g. *make a decision, clarify information*. Also elicit alternatives of similar meaning, e.g. *find a solution to a problem, solve a problem*.

> **Suggested answers**
> give or receive feedback, make a decision, find a solution to a problem, clarify previously received / given information, brainstorm ideas, agree on action

Skills book, Good business practice, Meetings, Opening a meeting, page 78

Listening 1 1

Explain that Ss are going to hear part of a meeting. Ss listen globally and establish the purpose of the meeting. Ss check their answers with a partner then check the answer with the whole group.

> To look at the different options for a performance-related pay scheme.

Listening 1 2

Explain that Ss are now going to focus on the language used to open the meeting. Refer Ss to the five steps and check comprehension. Ss listen and write the phrases used to introduce each step. Ss may need to listen several times. Allow Ss to check answers with a partner before you elicit answers from the whole group.

132

UNIT 4

> **Step 1:** Right – can we start?
> **Step 2:** Good morning, everyone. Thanks for coming to this meeting. Do you all know Harriet Blofeld, my new personal assistant?
> **Step 3:** Well – let me explain the background. As you know, …
> **Step 4:** Specifically, we've got three objectives: First …, Second …, And third…
> **Step 5:** Joanna, would you like to start by explaining the different options?

What do you say?

Explain that various phrases can be used for Steps 1–5. Ss match the phrases with the steps. Check Ss are comfortable with the pronunciation of the phrases.

1 e   2 b   3 d   4 c   5 a

> **Flexibility**
> Ways of working vary between cultures. People from different backgrounds have different expectations about what is normal, which may lead to tensions. For example, while it is dangerous to suggest stereotypes, German business people would typically expect to have fixed objectives for a meeting or project and would feel the need to know the constraints they might be working under. On the other hand, Saudi business executives might feel rather constrained by such a way of working and might prefer to use meetings to become comfortable with their business partners before signing any agreements. NB Ways of working may be affected by organisational culture as well as national culture.

Culture at work

Start this activity with Ss' books closed. Draw an empty spider diagram on the board with *Ways of working* in the middle. On each arm write a heading from the left of the Culture at work table on page 22. Ask Ss to approach the board and write in an appropriate place any thoughts / comments they have about cultural differences in the way people work. Explain that Ss may come into contact with people from different cultures with different expectations about ways of working, which may affect the effectiveness of the meetings they attend. (However, point out that it is dangerous to stereotype and that of course individuals vary.)

Now refer Ss to the table on page 22 then ask Ss to complete their own culture profile about fixed objectives or flexibility on page 82. (Ss identify and mark with a cross where they believe their culture is situated on the line ranging from Fixed objectives to Flexible working.) Collect Ss' responses and encourage a group discussion. You may wish to expand the discussion to incorporate any other issues that were raised on the spider diagram at the beginning of this section.

Skills book, Culture profile, page 82

Task 1

Ask Ss to read the problem at the bottom of Task 1 and check that they understand it. The meeting in Task 2 will be based on this topic.

Step 1: Divide the Ss into groups of 3–5. Ss follow the instructions and decide on their objectives for their meeting. Point out that each S should also decide an individual objective. Help the groups in their preparation as necessary.

Step 2: When the groups are ready, explain that they are going to report their objectives. Write the phrases from the book on the board and draw attention to the verb forms. Ensure Ss are confident with the use of the present perfect in the phrases *We've agreed …* and *I've decided …*. Also draw Ss' attention to:

We've agreed on + noun phrase   *We've agreed to* + infinitive
I've decided that + verb phrase   *I've decided to* + infinitive

See Language focus on the next page for differences between UK and US usage. Ask one person from each group to report back what they decided, using the key phrases on the board.

Skills book, Grammar reference: Present perfect and past simple, page 85

> **Optional activity**
> **Photocopiable resource 4.1 (page 178**
> This activity integrates practice of present perfect / past simple with a focus on cultural differences. Photocopy and distribute a worksheet to each S. Draw Ss' attention to the use of tenses: present perfect for the first general question followed by past simple for specific questions on where and when something happened. Ss work in pairs. Alternatively, allow Ss to mingle, asking one another questions in order to complete their worksheet. Ss feed back to the class any interesting information they have found. Draw Ss' attention to any grammatical errors and elicit corrections.

INTELLIGENT BUSINESS (INTERMEDIATE) TEACHER'S BOOK: SKILLS BOOK

> **Language focus: Present perfect in UK and US English**
>
> The present perfect is used much more in British English than in US English. Whenever there is a connection with the present, the present perfect is used in the UK. In the USA, the past simple tends to be used instead.
>
> *Have you sent out the agenda yet?* (UK)
> *Did you send out the agenda yet?* (US)
>
> *I've already done it.* (UK)
> *I did it already.* (US)

Self-assessment

Allow Ss a few minutes to think about what they have achieved from the unit and tick the boxes. Suggest what Ss can do to gain further practice.

- Video, Part 2
- CD-Rom

Task 2

If necessary, allow Ss a couple of minutes to remind themselves of the scenario from Task 1.

Step 1: Using the objectives they set in Task 1, in pairs, Ss plan how they will open the meeting. Refer Ss back to five steps from the listening exercise and the phrases they have met if necessary.

Step 2: Ss in each pair take turns to demonstrate the opening of their meeting. Ask a few Ss to demonstrate to the rest of the class.

Analysis, Task 2

Allow Ss a few minutes to reflect on the questions individually, then start a group discussion. Give your own feedback. Refer to effective language and any gaps / difficulties.

Step 3: Ss work in the same groups as Task 1. Ask Ss to choose a role or allocate one for them. Not all role cards are needed if numbers are small. Ask one S to lead the meeting and also express his / her own opinion based on the role card. Ss must bear in mind the objectives they set earlier. The focus is fluency; Ss should also be aware of their use of phrases to open a meeting and their use of present perfect / past simple. You may wish to record the meeting (audio or video) to enable Ss to assess themselves.

Task 3

In the same groups Ss decide whether they achieved their objectives. Refer Ss to the useful phrases on page 23, pointing out the use of the past simple. Collate some of the reactions.

Unit 5: Deal with problems

UNIT OBJECTIVES	
Skills:	Explain and clarify a problem Predict consequences Suggest and promise action
Language:	Modal verbs (*can, could, would, may, might*)
Culture at work:	Dealing with unclear situations

Speaking on the telephone is different to speaking in e.g. a meeting as the speakers cannot (generally) see one another. The following may be important, therefore, when on the telephone:
- Ensuring you give your name and the reason for the call
- Giving additional information to help the other person understand what is happening, e.g. *I'm just looking for my notes*
- Checking and clarifying that you have understood
- Summarising and being clear about any action to be taken.

Cultural attitudes may affect the following:
- The use of names (Some cultures, such as in Austria, place importance on the use of titles, such as *Herr Doktor Maier* rather than the use of first names)
- The amount of small talk at the beginning and end of the telephone conversation
- The day and time of day that it is acceptable to call (bearing in mind time zone differences)
- How problems are dealt with (See Culture at work).

What do you think?

Introduce the topic of the lesson: dealing with problems on the telephone. Ask students how often they use the telephone (how often they make a call and how often they receive one) and the kind of problems they might have. Collate ideas on the board concerning problems with phone calls. Refer Ss to the list of problems on page 24 and ask how Ss would deal with them. Ss match the problems with the expressions.

1 a c g i   2 a i   3 f g   4 b h j   5 e   6 b d e f

Skills book, Good business practice, Telephoning, Telephoning problems, page 80

Listening 1

Explain that Ss are going to hear a telephone call. Ensure that Ss understand the context: a Canadian company is going to start a controversial construction project in Africa. Ask Ss to listen to the first few sentences and focus on the language used at the beginning of a phone call. Ss answer the questions and check their answers with a partner before you check them. Get Ss to practise similar mini telephone dialogues before moving on to the rest of the listening.

a Is that Dan McGuire?
b Speaking
c Hello, Dan. This is Robert.

Listening 2

Now play the whole telephone conversation once. Do not give Ss a specific task. Instead, ask them to see if they can understand the general meaning of the conversation in preparation for the next exercise.

Task 1

Step 1: In pairs Ss try to explain the problem described in the phone call (above) and prepare any questions they could use to clarify the situation. Note some of Ss' questions on the board and check Ss are confident with the pronunciation and intonation.

Step 2: The pairs take turns to ask the rest of the group their questions.

> **Step 1:** Local farmers have changed their mind about the construction of the dam and are now protesting against it. Work is being held up as a result. If the army were brought in to move them, it would mean bad publicity for the company. If the company renegotiated the compensation paid to locals, it would delay the work and cost the company more money.
>
> **Step 2: Suggested questions**
> Can you clarify why some local farmers are protesting? Who are the foreigners who have joined the protest? Why doesn't the company want to bring in the army? Can you confirm your understanding of the action Dan is going to take?

What do you say?

Explain that there are different stages to any dialogue which focuses on dealing with a problem. Refer Ss to the list 1–5 and ask them to match one or more phrases with each stage. Check Ss' answers and that they are comfortable with the pronunciation of the phrases. Draw Ss' attention to the language used for predicting consequences in the exercise (*That'll result in ..., It could be ..., It'll mean ..., It might ...*). Write these on the board and focus on language for consequences that are likely to happen and consequences that are less likely to happen. (See Language focus below.)

| 1 g | 2 e | 3 b f i j | 4 a d | 5 c h |

Language focus: Predicting possible consequences

We can use the following to predict the consequences of an event that is likely to happen.

| It / That | 'll / may / could | mean ... |
| It / That | 'll / may / could | result in ... |

We can use the following to predict the consequences of an event that is less likely to happen.

| It / That | 'd / might / could | mean ... |
| It / That | 'd / might / could | result in ... |

We use *will* or *would* to express certainty. We use *may / might / could* to express uncertainty.

Culture at work

Ss work with books closed. Ss have just listened to a problematic or unclear situation and have looked at some language related to it. Explain that different cultures react to unclear situations in different ways: some try to avoid them in the first place; some accept they happen and deal with them. Write on the board the three headings from the left of the table on page 26. Divide the class into two groups. Ask one group to think about cultures that avoid unclear situations and the other group to think about cultures that tolerate them, and to think of what that might mean for that culture in terms of the three headings (*Rules, Precautions* and *Strategies*). You may need to give an example (e.g. give the first line from the table). Ask a speaker from each group to summarise their group's thoughts to the whole class. Now refer Ss to the table on page 26 and open up a group discussion. Does the other group agree? Do they have any experience of such situations themselves? How would they describe themselves? Then ask Ss to complete their own culture profile about dealing with unclear situations on page 82. (Ss identify and mark with a cross where they believe their culture is situated on the line ranging from Avoid unclear situations to Tolerate unclear situations.)

> Skills book, Culture profile, page 82

Task 2

Ss now have the chance to explain and clarify a problem in a role-play situation and predict the consequences of any action. Read the problem with the whole class. Ask questions about the ticket and email, e.g. *What time does Alex arrive in Barcelona? Where is the meeting going to be? Is it an important meeting? Why? / Why not?* Now divide the class into pairs and label each member Alex or Jo. Refer Ss playing Alex to page 98 and those playing Jo to page 26. Check they understand the situation. Allow Ss a few minutes to prepare, but discourage them from writing out their dialogue. Sit the pairs back-to-back to roleplay the situation. If possible, ask Ss to record themselves on a blank cassette. Make notes for feedback later.

Analysis, Task 2

Allow Ss a few minutes to reflect on the questions individually, then start a group discussion. Give your own feedback. Refer to effective language and any gaps / difficulties.

> Skills book, Grammar reference: Modal verbs: part 1, page 87

Task 3

Read the problem and the email with the whole group. Check comprehension. Elicit from Ss the language form used to promise action (*will*) and write some example sentences on the board, e.g. *I'll call the customer and tell them what's happened. I'll ask the driver to check for damage.* (See the Language focus sections on the next page.) Divide the Ss into pairs, ensuring that those Ss who were the caller (Alex) in Task 2 are the other role (Charlie) in this role-play. Refer the callers to page 100. Allow Ss a little time to prepare but tell them not to write a script. Ss carry out the telephone call back-to-back again. (If the group is small and circumstances allow, ask Ss to carry out the telephone conversations using real telephones in separate rooms.) Monitor Ss' performance, making notes on effective use of language.

UNIT 5

Language focus:
Suggestions and recommendations

We can use *shall* or could to make suggestions:
Shall *I call the customer?*
Perhaps we **could** *talk to them?*
Couldn't *we contact them?*

We do not use *to* with *suggest* or *recommend*. Notice the forms that we usually use.

Incorrect
~~We suggest / recommend **to take** the following action.~~

Correct
We suggest / recommend **taking** *the following action.*
We suggest / recommend **(that)** *you* **take** *the following action.*
We suggest / recommend **(that)** *the following action* **is taken**.

Language focus:
Promising action

We normally use *will* to promise action. The short form *'ll* is much more common in spoken language than the long form *will*.
I'll call you back soon. (spoken)
We'll try it out straight away. (spoken)
We **will** *make every effort to solve the problem immediately.* (written)

We can also use verbs which refer to the future.
We **plan** */* **expect** */* **hope** *to solve the problem immediately.*

Analysis, Task 3

Allow Ss a few minutes to reflect on the questions individually, then start a group discussion. Give your own feedback. Refer to effective language and any gaps / difficulties.

Self-assessment

Allow Ss a few minutes to think about what they have achieved from the unit and tick the boxes. Suggest what Ss can do to gain further practice.

- Video, Part 2
- CD-Rom

INTELLIGENT BUSINESS (INTERMEDIATE) TEACHER'S BOOK: SKILLS BOOK

Unit 6: Make a recommendation

UNIT OBJECTIVES

Skills:	Introduce a visual
	Compare alternatives
	Make a recommendation
Language:	Comparatives and superlatives
Culture at work:	Factual or vague?

Unit 3 focused on opening a presentation and general presentation skills. This unit builds on those skills and focuses on the effective use of visual aids. (Unit 8 of the Coursebook has a similar focus.) Using a presentation to make a recommendation may involve the following:
- Making your point clearly
- Using visual aids effectively
- Comparing alternatives
- Making a recommendation
- Cultural issues (both national culture and organisational culture).

Some language-related cultural considerations when using visuals in presentations are:
- Flexibility of what is said in relation to what is shown. (See Culture at work in Unit 3. Some presenters may use the visuals as a general stimulus for what is said; others may explain each visual systematically)
- Use of factual or vague language (See Culture at work in this unit)
- Formality of language (This will vary according to culture and situation).

What do you think? 1

Introduce the topic of the lesson: making a recommendation in a presentation and supporting your recommendation with visuals. Elicit what this may involve (see the first five bullet points in the box above). Explain that the first part of the lesson focuses on the effective use of visual aids. Draw a pie chart, a bar chart, a line graph and a table on the board and elicit the names. Ask students what kind of visuals they have used or would consider using in a presentation and why they would choose to use each particular type of visual. Note any key vocabulary on the board e.g. *pie chart, to compare, to make a comparison*. Refer Ss to the visuals on page 28. Ss match the visuals with the messages. Elicit the correct answers.

a 2   b 1   c 3

What do you think? 2

Then discuss the questions about the visuals. Note the Ss' use of the comparative and superlative in order to return to this area later. There are no correct answers. Ask Ss to give reasons for their choices.

> Skills book, Good business practice, Presentations, Using visuals in a presentation, page 77

Task 1

Refer Ss back to the sentences summarising the message of each visual on page 28. Then ask Ss to work in pairs and prepare a sentence about each of the charts on page 29. Elicit and compare Ss' sentences.

> **A:** The first chart shows a comparison of prices across three networks (Orange, O2 and Vodafone) of mobile phone calls to the UK from Australia, Spain and the USA.
> **B:** The second chart shows a comparison of prices across three networks (Orange, O2 and Vodafone) of text messages to the UK from Australia, Spain and the USA.

Task 2

Draw Ss' attention to the phrases for talking about visuals. Check Ss are comfortable with the pronunciation of the phrases and expand vocabulary so that they can talk about a range of visuals, e.g. *column, row* (referring to charts), *segment* (referring to pie charts), *line, point* (referring to line graphs). Then ask Ss to work in pairs again. Ask them to look at the information about Allsop Trading and to decide which of the alternative mobile phone providers Allsop should choose and why. After some time, ask one or two Ss to explain their choice, referring to the charts and comparing the alternatives. Note Ss' use of comparatives and superlatives in preparation for the next activity.

UNIT 6

Allsop will take a number of factors into account when choosing a mobile phone service provider. Their decision may take the following into account:
- From which countries do most staff contact the UK?
- Which is more common: phoning or texting?
- Can Allsop get a special deal (e.g. for bulk business) with one phone provider?

Since we do not know the answer to these questions, we can only point out the following:
- Texting is generally cheaper than phoning for all providers. Texting prices are roughly similar for all providers.
- One important thing to notice is that O2 telephone calls are more expensive than their competitors'. However, their text message service is often cheaper.
- In Chart A, we can see that phone calls from the USA are generally more expensive than phone calls from other countries. Orange offers the cheapest phone calls from the USA.
- If we look at the column on the right in Chart A, we notice that Vodafone's phone charges are higher than Orange's, except from Australia, where they are substantially cheaper.

> **Optional activity**
> **Photocopiable resource 6.1 (page 179)**
> If Ss need to review the formation of comparatives and superlatives, use this card matching activity. Prepare a set of cards for each pair or small group. Ss work in pairs or small groups and match the cards to make pairs; the result should be sentences that fit according to grammatical accuracy and meaning. Draw Ss' attention to the formation of comparatives and superlatives with:
> - *than* or *as*
> - single syllable adjectives and longer adjectives
> - adjectives ending in *–y*.
>
> Then write on the board any mistakes Ss have made with comparatives and superlatives during the lesson. Ask Ss to correct the mistakes.

Skills book, Grammar reference: Comparatives and superlatives, page 92

Listening 1

Explain that Ss are now going to hear a short presentation in which the telecommunications manager at Allsop compares the three alternatives. Ask Ss to listen to the CD and identify which supplier he chooses and whether he makes the same comments as they did. Play the CD more than once if necessary before eliciting answers.

Listening 2

Ss listen again and answer the questions. Elicit the correct answers.

> 1 Lee Jones recommends Vodaphone.
> 2 a So, in conclusion, I would recommend that we go with Vodaphone.
>   b He gives his reasons before he makes his recommendation. There are arguments for and against. Some would say before is more effective as the build-up leads to the recommendation. However, others would say the opposite approach is more effective by giving the audience something to link the reasons to, like a title on a page.

What do you say? 1

Check Ss understand what the table shows and point out the key. Elicit adjectives related to the nouns in the left-hand column:

Price – cheap / expensive
Weight – light / heavy
Image quality – good / bad
Time to download – quick / slow
Ease of use – easy / difficult.

Ask Ss to complete the sentences individually then compare in pairs. Give feedback to pairs.

> **Suggested answers**
> One advantage is that it offers the best image quality. Another is that it has more special features than the other two cameras.
> However, there is a slight disadvantage in that it is more expensive and heavier than the other cameras.
> But I would recommend the Snap Happy because it is cheapest, lightest and easiest to use of the three cameras. Also, the image quality is adequate for our needs.

What do you say? 2

Ask Ss to decide which camera they would choose to buy themselves and to be clear about their reasons. Allow Ss a couple of minutes to prepare to present their choice to their partner, but without writing a script. Ss present their choice, giving reasons by referring to the chart. Note the use of Ss' language to refer to visuals as well as their use of comparatives and superlatives. Give feedback to the class as a whole.

Culture at work

Ask Ss to read the information about factual and vague cultures. Ensure Ss understand the meaning of *modifiers* (i.e.

139

adverbs that modify adjectives, e.g. *it is **quite** high, it's **a bit** high, it's **much** higher, it's **a little** higher*). In order to check Ss' understanding of the concept, ask them to look at the pairs of sentences below the box and to identify which statement is factual and which is vague. Then ask Ss to think about their own culture in terms of factual or vague culture and to complete their own culture profile on page 82. (Ss identify and mark with a cross where they believe their culture is situated on the line ranging from Factual to Vague.) Ask Ss where they believe British culture is on this line. Point out that British speakers of English tend to use vague language, particularly when expressing criticism or disagreement. (See Language focus below.) Explain that when using English as an international language, it is useful to be sensitive to such differences between cultures. Failure to understand that another culture is more direct / factual than your culture (or the opposite) can lead to misunderstandings.

1 vague (*a bit, sometimes*)
2 factual (*four out of ten, more than 15 minutes*)
3 vague (*a little more*)
4 factual (*€60*)
5 factual (*two-thirds*)
6 vague (*most, seem to be, quite*)

Skills book, Culture profile, page 82

Language focus: Using vague language to express criticism

In British English it is rare to express criticism or disagreement directly. Instead, vague language is often used in order to be polite.

Meaning	British English
That's wrong.	*That isn't quite right.*
You made a mistake.	*There seems to have been a bit of a misunderstanding.*
It's too expensive.	*It's a bit too expensive for us.*
You're talking nonsense.	*I can't quite understand the reasons for your decision.*

Task 3

Step 1: Explain that Ss will now use the language they have covered in this unit to make a presentation. Give them ten minutes to prepare a short presentation with supporting visual(s). The presentation should include comparisons and a recommendation. It may be a good idea to take magazines and advertisements into the classroom (so that Ss can find three computers / cars / holidays etc. to compare). If Ss are going to present to the whole class, you may want to give them flipchart paper and pens, or OHP transparencies and pens.

Step 2: Ss present their comparison and recommendation to the group. Depending on time and individual Ss' ability, you might want to encourage the other Ss to ask the presenter questions. Note Ss' use of language, including their use of language referring to visuals, comparatives and superlatives, and vague or factual language.

> **Optional activity**
> You may want to extend the presentation task. If so, consider using the Presentation preparation and feedback frameworks on pages 186 and 187.

Analysis, Task 3

Allow Ss a few minutes to reflect on the questions individually, then start a group discussion. Give your own feedback. Refer to effective language and any gaps / difficulties.

Self-assessment

Allow Ss a few minutes to think about what they have achieved from the unit and tick the boxes. Suggest what Ss can do to gain further practice.

Skills book, Units 3, 8 and 14, pages 14, 38 and 66

Coursebook, Unit 8, page 73

Teacher's book, Presentation preparation framework, page 186

Teacher's book, Presentation feedback framework, page 187

Teacher's book, pages 60, 127, 146 and 168

Video, Part 2

CD-Rom

Writing 2: Memos

UNIT OBJECTIVES	
Skills:	Write a short memo
	Write a recommendation
Language:	Modal verbs / formal recommendations

Memos are used for internal communication. They are usually addressed to all staff or a particular group of staff; sometimes they can be used for formal communications addressed to an individual. They normally have headings showing who the memo is to and from and also a subject heading. They are not normally signed by the writer (though the writer may put his / her initials at the bottom). The word *memo* is short for *memorandum* (plural: *memoranda*); the longer form of the word is now rarely used. The following may be important when writing memos:
- The reader
- The purpose of the memo
- The structure of the memo and sequence of points
- Clarity, conciseness, consistency
- The level of formality (Although memos are used for internal communication and are mostly written in a neutral style, levels of formality vary)
- Tone (It is important to choose an appropriate tone, especially if giving bad news or reprimanding staff)
- Accuracy (grammar, spelling, punctuation).

Cultural attitudes (varying according to national culture and also organisational culture) may have an impact on the following:
- The extent to which memos are used and received
- Formality of language
- The tone of instructions or recommendations.

Style guide, Memos, page 22
Style guide, General rules, page 3
Style guide, Organising your writing, page 4
Teacher's book, Writing preparation framework, page 188
Teacher's book, Writing feedback framework, page 189

What do you think? 1

Introduce the topic of the session: writing memos. Ask Ss whether they write and / or receive memos, and if so to / from whom and for what purpose (to inform staff, to remind staff, to reprimand staff, to make a recommendation etc.). Check Ss are clear about who writes memos to whom. What do Ss think about the type of language that should be used in a memo? Would it be similar to language in an email? Ss look at the memo and comment on layout only. (Ss should not read the content at this stage.) Give feedback. Ensure Ss notice that memos can have the label *Memo* to ensure the identity of the document is clear. Draw Ss' attention to the *To / From / Subject* headings and the lack of a signature.

> There is a clear heading *Memo* to clarify the type of communication. The headings at the top are similar to an email (it is clear who the memo is for, who sent it and what the subject is). The body of the memo is divided into paragraphs.

What do you think? 2

Ss now read the memo, focusing on the content, and answer the questions.

> a the pay office
> b all staff
> c The payment of salaries will be delayed.
> d The company has a new computer system, which is causing problems and delays.
> e The problem will be solved in the next two or three days and payment will be made by the end of the month.

What do you think? 3

Ss then look at the language used in more detail and decide whether the memo is written in a formal or informal style. Write the following two categories on the board: *Vocabulary* and *Grammar* and elicit Ss' ideas. (See Language focus on the next page.) Point out that the memo uses the active rather than the passive as the company takes personal responsibility for finding a solution.

> The memo is neutral / slightly formal (e.g. use of *inform* rather than *tell*, and *we will make every effort* rather than *we will try*). It is definitely not informal. (See Language focus on formal language on the next page.)

INTELLIGENT BUSINESS (INTERMEDIATE) TEACHER'S BOOK: SKILLS BOOK

> **Language focus:**
> **Formal and informal language**
>
> | VOCABULARY | More formal | Less formal |
> |---|---|---|
> | Latin origin vs Germanic origin | inform
regret
delay | tell
be sorry
lateness |
> | Phrasal verbs | contact
solve | get in touch with
sort out |
>
> | GRAMMAR | More formal | Less formal |
> |---|---|---|
> | Long forms (f) | is not | isn't |
> | Noun phrases (f) | make every effort | try |
> | Passives (f) | will be delayed | we will delay |
> | Impersonal phrases (f) | there will be some delay in payment | we will delay payment |

Task 1

Ss now have the chance to write a memo. Refer Ss to the scenario and notes on page 32. Encourage Ss to use the memo on page 32 as a model in terms of layout, structure and functional language. Draw Ss' attention to functional language for promising future actions. Ss do the writing task. Encourage peer correction then give feedback. Before moving on to the next exercise, tell Ss that formal recommendations are often made in memos. Refer Ss to the final section on formal recommendations of the Grammar reference and to Exercise 2 on page 88. Ensure that Ss can promise future action and make recommendations appropriately. See the Language focus section on page 137 of this Teacher's book.

> **Suggested answer**
> **Memo**
> To: All staff
> From: General administration office
> Subject: Closure of canteen
> We regret to inform you that the canteen will be closed during the month of August. This is due to renovation work.
> We will make every effort to complete the work within four weeks and expect to be able to resume full service by the end of August.
> Thank you for your patience.

Skills book, Grammar reference: Modal verbs, part 2, page 88

What do you write?

If Ss have studied Unit 6, refer them back to the Allsop Trading scenario and Lee Jones' presentation (pages 29 / 30) comparing three mobile phone service providers and making a recommendation. If Ss have not studied Unit 6, set the scene. In both cases, elicit what aspects of a mobile phone service provider would be of interest to a company. Ask Ss to suggest appropriate headings for a memo from Lee Jones making a recommendation about choice of phone providers and write this on the board. (Ensure it is similar to that on page 33, part f.) Then refer Ss to the framework showing the structure of a memo and the jumbled sections of the memo sent by Lee. In pairs, Ss order the sections. Give feedback. Ss then read the memo and summarise why Lee recommends Vodaphone. Focus then on the language used, e.g. *I'm attaching* and elicit additional possible alternatives, e.g. *I attach, please find attached*.

> 1 f   2 c   3 d   4 e   5 a   6 b   7 g

Task 2

Ss now have the chance to write a memo. Ss look at the scenario on page 33 and the information about digital cameras on page 30. The scenario in Task 2 asks Ss to write a memo to a colleague; however, Ss may choose to write the memo to the colleague's department rather than to the individual. Alternatively, Ss choose another situation of their own. Encourage peer correction before you give your feedback.

> **Suggested answer**
> **Memo**
> To: Tom Salter, Website Team
> From: Sue Goode
> Subject: Recommendation for digital camera
> I was requested to suggest a digital camera for use in the production of web pages. I recommend choosing the Photo Art TF2. This is because of its excellent image quality.
> I have compared the features of three digital cameras: Pixel Tek 4000, Snap Happy and PhotoArt TF2. My findings are as follows.
> **Pixel Tek 4000:** Download times, ease of use and price are average. Image quality is relatively high. If budget is a consideration, this may be a possible option.
> **Snap Happy:** Download times, ease of use and price are excellent. However, image quality is not quite good enough for professional web use.
> **PhotoArt TF2:** The camera is expensive and rather slow and difficult to use at first. However, image quality is excellent, making it suitable for use in web development. The camera also has video and sound recording features but these are of insufficiently high quality for professional purposes.
> This comparison shows that the PhotoArt TF2 is the best buy for your purposes. I attach further information to support the recommendation.

Skills book, Unit 6, page 30

Unit 7: Brainstorm solutions

UNIT OBJECTIVES	
Skills:	Define the problem
	Make suggestions and respond
	Evaluate suggestions
Language:	Conditionals 1 and 2
Culture at work:	Decision-making

> Brainstorming aims to generate as many ideas on a given topic as possible by allowing people to suggest anything, however unrealistic it may seem. A brainstorming session generally works best if there is a facilitator, someone who encourages contributions and who collects the ideas. This person should take care not to affect the ideas in any way, such as by giving his / her own reaction to them. There are different ways of recording the ideas generated. Some companies / cultures use a flipchart or whiteboard; others use cards which can be grouped and pinned to a pinboard (known as Metaplan in Germany); others use mind maps. Note that some people avoid the term *brainstorming* as it can be used in a medical context to refer to a seizure; they prefer to use other terms such as *ideas storming* to refer to the spontaneous generation of ideas.
>
> Cultural attitudes may affect the following:
> - Willingness and speed in accepting that there is a problem which needs solving
> - Being prepared to propose suggestions and offer opinions on others' ideas
> - The decision-making process (see Culture at Work).

What do you think?

Introduce the topic of the lesson: brainstorming solutions. Before Ss open their books, elicit what might happen in a brainstorming meeting (during the brainstorming phase and afterwards). Write key ideas and vocabulary on the board, e.g. *generate ideas, be creative, value opinions, discuss advantages / disadvantages of the ideas, produce a shortlist, agree an action plan*. Ask Ss to open their books and ensure Ss understand the points in the list on page 34. In pairs Ss tick the points they agree with and change the wording of the other sentences so that they express their opinion. Encourage a group discussion if time.

Suggested answers
Ss may decide to amend points 3, 6 and 8 as follows:
3 It isn't necessary to have a leader at a brainstorming meeting – but it's necessary to have a facilitator (i.e. someone who makes sure that all ideas are heard and recorded but does not influence the opinions.
6 Don't discuss ideas until the brainstorming phase has finished.
8 Write down all ideas during the brainstorming phase. Don't evaluate the ideas until later.

> Skills book, Good business practice, Meetings, Holding a brainstorming meeting, page 78

Task 1

Explain that Ss will be listening to a brainstorming meeting. First, set the scene based on the case study on page 35: Springfield, a chain of department stores, has a problem; but do not say more about the problem at this stage. Ask Ss to read the case study individually. Ss should be able to guess the meaning of *to desert* from the context. Then Ss work in pairs to define the problem in two sentences using the prompts on page 34. Draw Ss' attention to two possible continuations of the phrase *the problem is ... :*

The problem is that + verb phrase
The problem is one of + noun phrase.

Give each pair a large piece of paper and pen, and then pin up Ss' answers on a board. Or during feedback, ask one S from each pair to write their definitions on the board. The class votes on the best definition of the problem and suggested solution.

Suggested answers
The problem is that Springfield's sales have fallen by 30%, they haven't made a profit for three years, and they are losing market share to smaller, more specialised, modern chains.
The company needs to define its strategy, focus the goods it sells according to its strategy and modernise its stores.

Listening (CD9)

Explain that Ss are going to hear the managers of Springfield brainstorming a solution to the problem. Before playing the CD, ask Ss what specific solutions they think the managers may suggest. Play the first extract (CD9) and, before Ss look at the questions, ask Ss to note down the ideas that are brainstormed (introduce more discount sales, close larger stores and relocate to smaller buildings in out of town locations, decorate stores in a more modern style, make the image more exciting). Then play the same extract again and ask Ss to answer the first two questions on page 35. During feedback, write the phrases on the board. Ask one or two Ss to say them, checking pronunciation.

> 1 He is not effective as a facilitator of a brainstorming session. He did not allow some ideas to be developed e.g. discount sales. He cut the speaker short.
> 2 He gave his personal opinion on each suggestion: But that's not good for profits. Our margins are low enough already!
> Hmm – that could save a lot of costs!
> Yes, that's a good idea. Do you think we should …?

Listening (CD10)

Play the second extract. This time the speakers also propose some different suggestions. What are they (change the displays more often, organise special events, e.g. fashion shows and celebrity visits)? Then play the second extract again for Ss to answer questions 3-5. Ask Ss to compare their answer with a partner then discuss answers with the class.

> 3 He kept his requests for ideas neutral. Sometimes he showed that he had heard a suggestion by simply repeating it, rather than commenting on it, and encouraging speakers to continue: So – any suggestions? So – any other ideas? Decorate the stores. OK – go on.
> 4 He explained the danger of evaluating each suggestion and what it would mean: If we stopped to evaluate each idea, it would take too long – and people wouldn't be as creative.
> 5 The leader / facilitator in the second extract was generally more effective in generating ideas. He requested ideas neutrally, did not give his own reaction to them, prevented other people from giving reactions, and encouraged the ideas to develop.

What do you say? Making suggestions

Ensure that Ss understand the meaning of *tentative*: a tentative statement or suggestion is one where the speaker does not appear confident it will be approved or accepted. We are often tentative if we think people may not accept our ideas. Also, in British English, tentativeness is often a sign of politeness. Write two forms of the same suggestion on the board and ask Ss which they think is a firm suggestion and which is a tentative suggestion.

Let's hold our lesson outside. (firm)
Perhaps we could hold our lesson outside. (tentative)

Explain that at the Springfield brainstorming meeting some people made firm suggestions and some made tentative ones. Ss look at the list on page 35 and tick the suggestions that are tentative. Check Ss' answers. Explain how suggestions can be made more tentative in English (see Language focus below) and practise the correct stress and intonation of the phrases with the Ss.

> The following are tentative:
> *What if we held some fashion shows?*
> *I don't suppose we could invite some celebrities?*
> *Perhaps we could decorate in a more modern style.*

Language focus: Tentative suggestions

We often express tentativeness in English by using a past form or Conditional 2. We can also use words to express possibility rather than certainty. Sometimes we use a negative form.

Firm suggestions
Let's change our image.
What if we change our image?

Tentative suggestions
*What if we **changed** our image?*
*One possibility **would** be to change our image.*
***Perhaps** we **could** change our image.*
*It **might** be a good idea if we **changed** our image.*
*I **don't suppose** we could change our image?*

Responding to suggestions

Now focus on language for responding to suggestions. Ss look at the list of phrases and identify neutral phrases.

> The following phrases are neutral: OK. Any other ideas?
> Right – I've got that. What else?
> Other possible neutral phrases are: Go on. Carry on.
> Could you say a bit more about that? Can you expand on that? Can you give us some details?

Task 2

Ss now have the chance to practise brainstorming themselves. Explain that they are going to brainstorm the Springfield problem and the pictures may suggest some ideas. Look at the pictures with the whole class, making sure they are clear what each represents (1 crèche facilities so parents can leave their children while they shop, **2** special event at the store to attract children, **3** shopping from home by credit card, **4** celebrity event, e.g. demonstration by a famous chef. Ask one S to be the facilitator and make sure he / she understands what to do. Ss brainstorm their ideas. NB: Ss will need their suggestions for Task 3 so ensure the facilitator notes down all the ideas. It may be easiest to give the facilitator some flipchart paper so that you can continue to use the board before Task 3. Make notes so that you can give your feedback after Task 2 Analysis.

Analysis, Task 2

Allow Ss a few minutes to reflect on the questions individually, then start a group discussion. Give your own feedback.

Culture at work

Ask Ss to work with their books closed. Write each point from the Culture at work table on page 37 on a separate piece of paper. Ask Ss to sort the papers into two groups – Individualist and Group cultures. Ss check their answers by looking in their books. Ask Ss why they grouped the items as they did and where they think their own culture fits. They then complete the culture profile.

Skills book, Culture profile, page 82

Task 3

Ensure Ss understand the meaning of *evaluate*. Write the following suggestion on the board: *What if we held our lesson outside?* Then elicit some comments evaluating the suggestions, e.g. *If we held our lesson outside, we'd get some fresh air. But, we might not learn much because we could get distracted.* Point out that it is common – but not necessary – to use Conditional 2 when evaluating suggestions (see Language focus below). Review the form and use of Conditional 2 if necessary. (You may wish to do the optional activity using photocopiable resource 7.1 at this stage – see below.) When Ss are confident about the language they can use to evaluate suggestions, refer Ss back to their list of suggestions for Springfield from Task 2. First Ss group them into three or four categories, then they evaluate the suggestions and lastly they decide which three are the best ideas. Point out the questions on page 37 and ask Ss to discuss each idea. Are Ss happy to agree on one or more specific solutions?

Skills book, Grammar reference: Conditionals 1 and 2, page 89

Language focus: Evaluating suggestions

We often use Conditional 2 to comment on or evaluate a suggestion. This is because the suggestion has not yet been accepted as definite.

Suggestion	Comment
Perhaps we could try to change our image.	*It'd be quite a risky decision to take.*

We can use *might* and *could* to express uncertainty in Conditional 2 sentences.

Suggestion	Comment
What if we tried to change our image?	*That might / could be dangerous.*

Sometimes we use complete Conditional 2 sentences to discuss proposals:
If we did that, our margins would be lower.

Optional activity
Photocopiable resource 7.1 (page 179)

Photocopy and give a worksheet to each S. Ss work in pairs and take turns to make tentative suggestions from the prompts. Ss make a brief comment on each other's suggestions, using Conditional 2, e.g. *It wouldn't work, That might be risky, If we did that, it'd mean ....*

Suggested answers
1 If we invested more in advertising, we could increase sales.
2 It might be a good idea if you didn't mention your concerns.
3 What if we reconsidered the price?
4 Perhaps we could wait for your colleague to return.
5 One possibility would be to bring forward the delivery date.
6 I don't suppose I could discuss the idea with my team first?
7 They might accept the offer if you delivered free of charge.
8 We might be able to start work straight away if we agreed on a letter of intent.

Analysis, Task 3

Allow Ss a few minutes to reflect on the questions individually, then start a group discussion.

Self-assessment

Allow Ss a few minutes to think about what they have achieved from the unit and tick the boxes. Suggest what Ss can do to gain further practice.

Video, Part 3

CD-Rom

INTELLIGENT BUSINESS (INTERMEDIATE) TEACHER'S BOOK: SKILLS BOOK

Unit 8: Get attention

UNIT OBJECTIVES

Skills: Open the presentation
Speak with emphasis
Refer to visuals
Language: Adjectives and adverbs and the language of change
Culture at work: Formal and informal presentations

Units 3 and 6 have already introduced some skills related to giving a presentation. This unit builds on those. (Units 3, 8 and 14 of the Coursebook also focus on presentations.) When opening a presentation, it is important to gain the audience's attention immediately. In order to do this, consider use of the following:
- Clear language
- Adjectives and adverbs to add emphasis
- The 'tripling effect' (saying things in threes, e.g. *It's fast, flexible and effective*)
- Stress (using your voice to stress key ideas and words)
- Audience involvement (e.g. by asking questions).

Cultural attitudes may affect the way in which attention is attracted in a presentation, e.g.
- The level of directness at the beginning of the presentation
- The use of humour as opposed to giving straight facts

Culture may also affect the level of formality of the language used and of the dress code of the presenter.

What do you think?

Introduce the topic of the lesson: getting attention in a presentation. Ask Ss if they have given a presentation or have spoken in public. If so, how did they get the audience's attention? If not, what ideas do they have? Collect key vocabulary on the board, e.g. *introduction, visuals, script, enthusiasm, clarity*. Refer Ss to the list on page 38. Ss tick the strategies they would use. Collect answers and open up a group discussion.

> Use simple language with short sentences. Show colourful visuals. Be enthusiastic. Keep eye contact with the audience. Ask questions from time to time.

Skills book, Good business practice, Presentations, Delivering a presentation, page 76

Listening 1 [1]

Explain that Ss will now have the chance to hear three ways of catching the audience's attention in the first few sentences. Refer Ss to the three strategies on page 39, play the CD and Ss match each one with an example. Check the answers. Ss then turn to the audioscript and underline useful phrases for each strategy:

Giving an interesting fact or statistic: *I've got some very good news for you, I expect you'd like to see the details, Right – so let me show you …*

Showing why your presentation is relevant: *I know that many of you here today …, And you would like to know if …, Well, I'm going to …, I think you'll find them interesting*

Asking the audience a question: *How many people here have …? Have you seen …? I'd like to tell you about …*

Stress and intonation can also help attract an audience's attention. Play the CD again and ask Ss to listen and mark the stress in the phrases. Ask them to listen again and notice the intonation. Ss repeat the phrases quietly to themselves. Then ask a few Ss to demonstrate to the class. This will be revisited in Task 2.

a 2   b 3   c 1

Listening 1 [2]

In pairs, Ss discuss what presenters in their company / country do in order to get attention at the start of a presentation and which style they prefer. Answers will depend on Ss' own experiences.

Task 1

In pairs, Ss choose one of the situations and thinks of an interesting way to open the presentation. Encourage different pairs to choose different situations. Ss practise in pairs. One person from each pair then demonstrates their opening to the rest of the class. Make notes.

Analysis, Task 1

Ask the whole class about the strategies each pair used and whether it made them want to hear the rest of the presentation. Give additional feedback on the presentations (e.g. regarding language accuracy and effectiveness) using the notes you made earlier.

146

Culture at work

Ss work with books closed. In small groups, Ss brainstorm what they think makes a presentation formal or informal. Give feedback to the whole class and refer Ss to the table on page 39. Does it suggest the same things as they came up with? Can they expand the information, e.g. what would be considered casual dress? Can they demonstrate tightly controlled body language? Can they think of an example of humour they have heard or used in a presentation? Can they produce a sentence with two versions – one with elaborate expressions, the other with everyday expressions? Generate a discussion about the Ss' own culture(s). Then ask Ss to complete their own culture profile in this area on page 82. (Ss identify and mark with a cross where they believe their culture is situated on the line ranging from Formal presentations to Informal Presentations. You may wish to ask Ss to write two marks on the line: a cross indicating their organisational culture, and a circle indicating the culture in general in their country.)

Skills book, Culture profile, page 82

What do you say? 1

Link this to the previous section by explaining that the way different cultures refer to numbers can vary: some cultures value specific facts and figures; others give approximate figures only so that the audience can grasp the big picture easily, ignoring the detail. Ensure that Ss understand *to round up* and *to round down*. Before Ss look at their books, write the numbers from the left-hand column of page 40 on the board. Ask individual Ss to volunteer to say them. Correct as necessary. Ask Ss whether they would give such exact figures in a presentation. Or would they round them up / down, and if so how? Refer Ss to page 40. Ss match the exact figures with their approximations. Check answers. Focus on language used for approximations: *approximately, roughly, about, nearly, almost*.

a 4   b 8   c 2   d 1   e 6   f 5   g 3   h 7

What do you say? 2

Focusing on the language in the right-hand column, Ss decide which expressions suggest a small amount. Give feedback.

only, (just) under

What do you say? 3

Focusing on the language in the right-hand column, Ss decide which expressions suggest an amount is too much. Point out that *just*, indicating a small degree, can be used in *just under / over* with a small or large amount. Ask Ss to use some of the vague language studied by giving figures relating to their own work or study.

more than, (just) over

Optional activity

Write pairs of numbers on the board, e.g.

249,000	*250,000*
98.77	*101*
1,000,050	*999,999*
33.32%	*24.6%*

Elicit a sentence about each pair, involving a noun, verb and an approximate description, e.g. *The value of the investment **went up** from just under a quarter of a million to a quarter of a million exactly.* You may first want to elicit synonyms or near synonyms of *went up: increased, rose, climbed* etc., then of *went down: decreased, declined, fell* etc.

Optional activity
Photocopiable resource 8.1 (page 180)

Another possibility for reviewing language of change is to do a card sorting activity. Photocopy the cards and give a set to each pair. First ask Ss to sort the verbs into three groups: up, down and no change. Ss find corresponding nouns, where appropriate. Then ask Ss to decide what type of movement is expressed by the adjectives and adverbs. Ask about size and speed of change (e.g. *dramatic* usually refers to a large fast change). Ss then match nouns and verbs with adjectives and adverbs and make correct sentences.

Skills book, Grammar reference: Adjectives and adverbs and the language of change, page 93

Listening 2 1

Ss keep their books closed. Explain that Ss will now hear part of a presentation about PDAs and Smartphones. Check that they know what these are. If any Ss possess such items, ask them to explain or demonstrate if applicable. Play the CD once, asking Ss to draw a simple graph on a piece of paper to represent what is happening to PDAs and what is happening to Smartphones (approximately). Give feedback. (Sales of PDAs = constant, sales of Smartphones = rising.) Ss now open their books and look at the text on page 40. Link this activity with the previous section by asking Ss to identify the numbers mentioned; draw attention to the way in which numbers are phrased. Then, following the examples in the text, Ss listen and underline the stressed words. Check Ss' answers.

INTELLIGENT BUSINESS (INTERMEDIATE) TEACHER'S BOOK: SKILLS BOOK

Listening 2 **2**

Ss now mark the pauses as they listen. To allow Ss to check their answers, play the CD again. Stress the importance of speaking with appropriate stress and pauses when trying to make an effect in a presentation.

> The handheld computer is <u>dead</u>, ‖ and the <u>future</u> is in <u>Smartphones</u>. ‖ How do I <u>know</u>? ‖ Just <u>look</u> at the <u>figures</u>. ‖ As you can <u>see</u>, ‖ sales of <u>PDAs</u> have stayed <u>flat</u> at around <u>eleven</u> million units <u>worldwide</u>. ‖ What about sales of <u>Smartphones</u>? ‖ They're rising <u>fast</u> ‖ from just <u>four</u> million <u>last</u> year ‖ to nearly <u>twelve</u> million <u>this</u> year.
> The PDA <u>market</u> will never be a <u>mass</u> market. ‖ Almost <u>everyone</u> who wants a <u>PDA</u> now <u>has</u> one.

Language focus: Speaking with emphasis

Words carrying key information are generally stressed. These are often nouns and verbs. However, depending upon the message being communicated, there are also instances when adjectives and adverbs can be stressed, e.g.
*Last year sales increased **slowly**. This year they have increased **rapidly**.*

Pausing can also add impact to what you are saying. In the first sentence of Listening 2 for example, the pause makes the contrast between the two phrases very obvious.

Task 2

Step 1: To review and rehearse speaking with emphasis, ask some Ss to read the text from Listening 2 to the whole group, or work in small groups if the class is large. Monitor and provide feedback.

Step 2: Then ask Ss to focus on a new text: the script on technology spending in the USA. Encourage Ss to decide what is important information in the text, which parts they want to draw the audience's attention to and only then mark the stress. Ss also decide on the pauses they wish to insert. Ss mark the script as they did in Listening 2 and practise speaking with emphasis. Monitor. Ss could be audio-recorded to enable them to do the analysis more effectively. Ask confident Ss to present their script in front of the whole class as this will bring out the instinct to 'act it up'. You could draw Ss' attention to the phrase used to draw the audience's attention to the visual (*if you look at the graph, it's clear that ...*) and elicit other possibilities, e.g. *as you can see ..., you'll notice that, this part of the graph clearly shows that ...* .

Suggested answer

<u>Technology spending</u> by <u>US companies</u> ‖ goes in long-term <u>cycles</u>. ‖ If you <u>look</u> at the <u>graph</u>, ‖ it's clear ‖ that <u>big leaps</u> in <u>new technology</u> ‖ happen roughly every <u>15</u> years. ‖ This <u>leads</u> ‖ to a <u>spending boom</u>, ‖ <u>followed</u> by a relative <u>calm</u>. ‖ Right now ‖ spending is <u>increasing</u> ‖ – but only ‖ by <u>two</u> per cent. ‖ In the <u>late 1990s</u>, ‖ growth was ‖ <u>11</u> per cent. ‖ While back in the <u>early 80s</u>, ‖ it was as high as ‖ <u>16</u> per cent.

Analysis, Task 2

Allow Ss a few minutes to reflect on the questions individually and listen to their recordings (if there are any). Then start a group discussion. Give your feedback.

Task 3

Ss now have the chance to bring everything together: language of change, talking about numbers, speaking with emphasis and opening a presentation. If time is tight, Step 1 of Task 3 could be set as homework and Step 2 done in the next lesson.

Step 1: Ss choose one of the graphs on page 103, or Ss in work may prefer to use their own graphs. First they prepare by finding appropriate language, then they should prepare an interesting opening that will catch the audience's attention. Encourage Ss to mark the stressed words and pauses on their script.

Step 2: In small groups and using the phrases provided, Ss open their presentation and refer to the visual. They should aim to describe trends while keeping the audience's interest. The presentations could be audio or video recorded to enable peer or self-evaluation.

Task 3, Analysis

Allow Ss a few minutes to reflect on the questions individually, then start a group discussion. Give your own feedback. Refer to effective language and any gaps / difficulties.

Self-assessment

Allow Ss a few minutes to think about what they have achieved from the unit and tick the boxes. Suggest what Ss can do to gain further practice.

- Skills book, Units 6 and 14, pages 28 and 66
- Coursebook, Units 3, 8 and 14, pages 29, 73 and 125
- Video, Part 3
- CD-Rom

Unit 9: Make small talk

UNIT OBJECTIVES	
Skills:	Introduce topics
	Keep it moving
	End politely
Language:	Questions
Culture at work:	Attitudes to personal space

When socialising, it is important to consider the following:
- Finding a topic of conversation that everybody feels comfortable with
- Not only starting a conversation, but also keeping it going (e.g. by showing interest and asking questions)
- Responding appropriately to what you hear
- Ending the conversation politely.

Cultural attitudes may have an impact on the following:
- The amount of time spent on small talk
- The topics of conversation that are considered 'safe' or not
- The boundaries of personal space (see Culture at work).

What do you think? 1

Introduce the topic of the lesson: small talk and socialising. Ask Ss if they enjoy socialising in a foreign language, e.g. English. Many of them will not enjoy it. Link their comments to the introduction to the unit. Point out that some preparation of socialising phrases and small talk topics in English may help Ss to feel less anxious when socialising. Draw a spider diagram on the board and write *small talk* in the middle. Ask Ss in which business situations they would need to make small talk. Ss will probably come up with at lunch, before and after a meeting etc. Then ask Ss to suggest topics of conversation, and add them to the spider diagram. If Ss suggest any topics that may cause offence to others, say so, adding brackets around the topic on the board. If Ss do not suggest any offensive topics, elicit some. Now refer Ss to page 42 and check comprehension by asking for examples of the topics in the lists, e.g. specific social problems. Discuss with the whole class.

Suggested answers
Safe topics: hobbies or special interests, films, sport (although in some cultures some women are discouraged from taking part in sports), travel, art and architecture, climate, food / customs. All the other topics may be fine in some cultures / situations but may cause offence in others.

What do you think? 2

Add any suggestions regarding safe or offensive topics to the spider diagram on the board.

Suggested answers
Additional safe topics: work / business, the town / area / current surroundings
Additional unsafe topics: business scandals / office gossip / ethical issues

Skills book, Good business practice, Socialising, Good business relations, page 81

Listening 1

Explain that Ss will hear two social conversations, one at lunch and one after a meeting. Ask Ss to predict what the people will talk about in both. Then play the CD and ask Ss to check to see whether their predictions were correct or not.

Conversation 1: the restaurant, jazz
Conversation 2: travel, Paul's journey home, traffic and commuting to work

Listening 2

Ss listen to the first conversation again in more detail and answer the questions.

a She makes a comment: It's a lovely restaurant! It's so big, but it feels friendly somehow.
b Oh, really? I can imagine!
c He asks a question: Do you like jazz?
d What about you?

Listening 3

Ss now listen to the second conversation again and answer the questions.

> a He asks a question: *Are you travelling back tonight?*
> b *You're lucky!*
> c He repeats the information that has surprised him: *An hour!*
> d Milo was polite. His excuse was that he was expecting a phone call and had to prepare for it: *Well, if you'll excuse me, I'm going to leave you with Mia.*

What do you say? Useful responses

Explain that it is useful to learn a number of standard fixed expressions that can be used when socialising. This includes words and phrases for responding to good, bad and surprising news. Ss match each response with a piece of news. Note that there are some instances where more than one match is possible. Check Ss' answers and elicit or offer other possibilities. Ensure Ss are comfortable with the intonation of the phrases (see Language focus below).

> 1 c d   2 c   3 a e f   4 b f   5 a b e f   6 a e

> **Language focus:**
> **Intonation when responding to news**
>
> It is important to respond to other people's news as silence can be misinterpreted. Useful phrases are:
>
> Good news: *Congratu<u>la</u>tions! That's a<u>ma</u>zing! Fan<u>tas</u>tic!*
> Bad news: *That's too <u>bad</u>! How <u>terr</u>ible!*
> Surprising news: *That's <u>in</u>teresting! That's a<u>ma</u>zing!*
>
> Intonation needs to match the meaning of what is being said; otherwise the speaker risks sounding ironic. Generally, when responding to news, intonation reaches a peak on the main stress and falls after that. It is also common to respond simply by saying *Really*; this response can be used in a wide variety of situations. Another option, if the speaker cannot think of what to say, is simply to make a noise, e.g. *Mmmm*, using the appropriate intonation.

Practice

In small groups, Ss prepare good, bad and surprising news. Ss take it in turns to give the news and respond. Monitor the appropriateness of Ss' responses and their intonation. Make the point that responding appropriately is one way to keep a conversation moving – but it is not enough. What other ways can Ss think of for keeping a conversation moving? Elicit the fact that it is also useful to use a range of question types. See Language focus below.

> **Language focus: Questions**
>
> It is very useful to use questions when socialising. They can be used for the following purposes.
>
> | | |
> |---|---|
> | To introduce a topic | *How long have you lived in Amsterdam?* |
> | To follow up and find out more | *Whereabouts* (= where exactly) *do you live?* |
> | To throw the conversation back to the other person | *What about you? / How about you? / And you?* |
>
> Different question forms can be useful for different reasons.
>
> | | |
> |---|---|
> | Closed (Yes / No) questions | are useful when starting a conversation. |
> | Open (Wh- / How) questions | are useful for developing the conversation. |
> | Polite (indirect) questions | are less intrusive than direct questions. |
> | Question tags: | pass responsibility for continuing the conversation to the other speaker. |

Skills book, Grammar reference: Questions, page 86

> **Optional activity**
> **Photocopiable resource 9.1 (page 180)**
> Play a game of dominoes and use this to lead into a focus on questions. Photocopy and distribute the dominoes. Ss look at the form of the questions (closed, open, polite, tag) and match the cards in a domino effect. If done correctly, a circle can be formed.
>
> **Answers**
> Does your company export? Where do you live? And you? Do you mind if I ask what the standard of living is like? It's an interesting conference, isn't it? How long have you worked for IBM? You'll give my regards to Sue, won't you? Would you mind if I spoke to your boss? What about your staff? How did you get here?

What do you say? Endings

To lead in to the exercise, refer back to the end of the last conversation. Can Ss remember how the speakers ended it? *(It's been very good meeting you. Thanks very much for coming.)* Ss now match more sentences for ending a conversation with the corresponding situation. Give feedback and talk Ss through common ways of ending a conversation in English (see Language focus on the next page). Ask Ss to work in pairs and prepare mini-dialogues in which they lead up to and end conversations in the three situations.

> 1 b   2 c   3 a

> **Language focus: Ending a conversation**
>
> When ending a conversation, we often express regret that it has to stop. Note that *I'm sorry* is followed by *but*; *I'm afraid* is not followed by *but*.
> *I'm sorry but I've got to get back to work.*
> *I'm afraid I've got to go now.*
>
> We usually say something positive when ending.
> *It's been good / nice talking to you.*

Task 1

Ss are going to do three tasks in which they introduce a topic (Task 1), keep the conversation moving (Task 2) and end the conversation (Task 3). Divide Ss into pairs, A and B. For Task 1, each S should choose two topics from the lists on pages 99 and 102. Each then takes turns to start a conversation. Remind Ss that it is common to start conversations either by making a comment (or making a comment and adding a question tag) or asking a question. The focus is on starting a conversation but encourage Ss to try to continue the conversation for a few exchanges.

Analysis, Task 1

In the same pairs, Ss discuss how effective they were at introducing the topics. If Ss were comfortable when introducing topics but not when continuing the conversation, use this as a lead-in to Task 2.

Task 2

Once a conversation has been started, it can be difficult to keep it moving. Emphasise the importance of responding appropriately rather than letting comments be followed by silence. Also remind Ss of the value of different types of questions. Stress that Ss should use strategies that put responsibility onto the other person (e.g. tag questions, open questions, follow-up questions, 'throw it back' questions); this will allow them thinking time. Ask Ss to start new conversations using the remaining topics from pages 99 and 102 or by choosing topics themselves. If the class is small, you may want Ss to record their conversations.

Analysis, Task 2

Allow Ss a few minutes to reflect on the questions individually (and listen to their recordings if done) then start a group discussion. Give your own feedback.

Culture at work

While culture can have an impact on the language we use, there are also non-verbal issues that need to be taken into account. Ensure that Ss realise that one of the purposes of small talk is to make people comfortable so that a successful business relationship can develop. It is important not to damage this relationship unintentionally by intruding on other people's personal space. Refer Ss to the text and table on page 45. Where would they put their own culture? Are they personally typical of their culture? Do Ss have any experience of situations where they have noticed differences between cultures? How did they feel when in a social situation with a differing culture? Can they advise on how to deal with the differences? Then ask Ss to complete their own culture profile about attitudes to personal space on page 82.

Skills book, Culture profile, page 82

Task 3

Ss now have the chance to bring everything together: to introduce and keep a conversation going, using safe topics, responding appropriately, ending politely and considering personal space. Divide the class into groups of 3–4 Ss and refer them to the three situations. Ss in each group need to represent two different companies, and they should discuss which company they belong to and who they are before they start. They can either play themselves, or adopt a new identity. They then keep this identity for all three situations. Ss start the first scenario. Give a signal (e.g. ring a bell) after a few minutes for Ss to move on to the next scenario. Monitor Ss' performance.

> **Optional activity**
> **Photocopiable resource 9.2 (page 181)**
> If Ss have difficulties coming up with ideas for Task 3, photocopy and distribute the role cards. There is additional information for both partners for each of the three situations.

Analysis, Task 3

Allow Ss a few minutes to reflect on the questions individually, then start a group discussion. Give your own feedback.

Self-assessment

Allow Ss a few minutes to think about what they have achieved from the unit and tick the boxes. Suggest what Ss can do to gain further practice.

Video, Part 3

CD-Rom

INTELLIGENT BUSINESS (INTERMEDIATE) TEACHER'S BOOK: SKILLS BOOK

Writing 3: Short factual reports

UNIT OBJECTIVES	
Skills:	Report trends
	Comment on the figures
Language:	Linking sentences and ideas – relative clauses

The following may be important when writing short factual reports:
- The reader (What is their relationship to the writer? What is their level of knowledge of the subject and their level of English?)
- The purpose of the report
- The structure of the report
- Clarity, conciseness, consistency
- The level of formality
- Accuracy (grammar, spelling, punctuation).

Cultural attitudes (varying according to national culture and also organisational culture) may have an impact on the following:
- The use of and format of reports
- Formality of structure and language.

Companies tend to have their own specific requirements regarding the structure of short reports. The same person may write a number of reports in different formats for different purposes and readers.

- Style guide, Short reports, page 26
- Teacher's book, Short reports, page 73
- Teacher's book, Writing preparation framework, page 188
- Teacher's book, Writing feedback framework, page 189

What do you think? 1

Introduce the topic of the session: writing short factual reports. Ask Ss whether they write and / or read factual reports, and if so what they are about. If not, what kind of facts do Ss think they could be used to report on? Explain that short reports often give or comment on figures. If possible, before the lesson, collect examples of graphs, lists of figures, pie charts etc. and show these to Ss to elicit relevant vocabulary. Alternatively, refer to Unit 8. Elicit key vocabulary: *trends, graphs, figures (actual and target), forecast*. You may also wish to revise other vocabulary relating to describing trends (e.g. *fluctuate, decrease, remain constant*). Now focus on the style of reports. Ss decide which of the options are better in a short factual report. Give feedback. Point out that even formal reports may make use of short simple sentences. As long as ideas between sentences are linked using linking words and phrases, the report will flow well. Reports may also contain longer sentences, but these should be divided into manageable chunks with ideas linked through the use of linking words and relative clauses.

a points organised under headings
b short simple sentences
c focus on key points only

What do you think? 2

Refer Ss to the chart on page 46 and ask one or two simple comprehension questions e.g. *What were the target sales for X5 in January? What were the actual sales of X5 in January?* Ss then complete the paragraph from a factual report describing the chart.

1 increased steadily
2 were just below target
3 were above target
4 an increase

Task 1

Point out that the forecast for X7 is smaller because newer models are expected to come on the market in spring. Then ask Ss to write similar short paragraphs for Products X6 and X7. You may wish to divide the class into smaller groups, asking some sub-groups to focus on X6 and the others on X7. The groups then exchange papers and comment on the others' work. Give feedback to the whole class.

In the next exercise (on page 47) Ss are going to move onto slightly more complex language of reports, where ideas are linked (commenting, showing consequences etc.). Review the use of linking words if necessary, referring Ss to the Grammar reference and exercises on page 95. Also briefly review relative clauses. (See Language focus on the next page.)

WRITING 3

Suggested answer

Product X6
Sales of X6 fluctuated through the first quarter. Sales were just below target in January. They decreased further in February, but then increased and were above target in March. We forecast overall sales to remain constant at around 1350 in the second quarter.

Product X7
Sales of X7 decreased steadily through the first quarter. Although actual sales were better in January than expected, they declined steadily in February and March, falling below target. The forecast for Quarter 2 reflects this decline. As X7 is an old model and newer models come on to the market in spring, we consequently expect Q2 sales to drop to approximately 750.

Language focus: Commenting on figures

We can use short simple sentences when commenting on figures and trends.
The total fell to 550,000. This was an improvement on the previous year.

Alternatively, we can link ideas in one sentence, using a relative clause. It is important to separate this clause with a comma (since it simply adds extra information).
The total fell to 550,000, which was an improvement on the previous year.

Skills book, Grammar reference: Linking sentences and ideas, page 95

What do you write?

Ss are now going to look at a slightly more complex short report. First ask Ss if they have been to a Mediterranean island. When do Ss expect tourist numbers to rise / peak / fall / reach a low point in such an island? Refer Ss to the graph on page 47 and focus Ss on the three lines indicating this year, last year and the previous year. Elicit a description of the lines on the graph, writing key vocabulary on the board (*rise, peak, disappointing* etc.) Check Ss understand the vocabulary above the graph. Now point Ss to the report under the graph. In pairs Ss fill the gaps with the vocabulary from the box. If time is short, divide the class into four groups, asking each group to focus on one paragraph of the report. Check Ss' answers. Before moving on to the next exercise, ask Ss to focus on the linking words and phrases in the report. Divide this into two steps:

1 Ask Ss to underline any comments on trends or figures using *this* or *which*. (*This* is used to add comments when describing the first, second and fourth quarters. *Which* is used to add comments in the third and fourth quarters.)

2 Ask Ss to circle any other linking words and phrases; they then identify which are used to refer to consequence (*so*) and which to refer to contrast (*however*). If necessary, remind Ss how to use the linking words and provide extra practice.

2 well
4 over
6 failed to reach
8 an improvement
10 poor

3 a disappointing month
5 significant
7 only
9 the normal pattern

Task 2

Ss now have the chance to write a short factual report, describing the third line on the graph and basing their report on the previous exercise. They should aim to organise their report logically under headings, and focus on key points, adding comments. They should use short sentences or longer sentences divided into chunks, and link ideas using linking words and phrases, Weaker Ss may wish to work in pairs. Ask Ss to show their writing to the other Ss for peer correction. If computers and a projector are available, Ss should type their report using a computer. Give your feedback on the Ss' writing.

Suggested answer

First quarter
We saw a promising start to the year, with tourist numbers rising to over 250,000 in March. This compared well with the same period the previous year.

Second quarter
Numbers in April remained constant followed by a slight increase in May. Although the trend was upward, these figures remained below the corresponding figures for the previous year.

Third quarter
Tourist numbers then rose and finally exceeded the previous August's figures, reaching a peak of 700,000, which was very pleasing. However, the number fell rapidly to just over 400,000 in September. This was due to bad weather.

Fourth quarter
Tourist numbers continued to drop towards the end of the year, which is the normal pattern. In October and November, numbers remained above the previous year, falling to the same level only in December.

Optional activity
You may want to extend the writing task. If so, consider using the Writing preparation and feedback frameworks on pages 188 and 189.

INTELLIGENT BUSINESS (INTERMEDIATE) TEACHER'S BOOK: SKILLS BOOK

Unit 10: Present an argument

UNIT OBJECTIVES	
Skills:	Give reasons
	Stress key words
	Present a structured argument
Language:	Linking sentences – cause and effect linkers
Culture at work:	Showing feelings

When presenting an argument (in a presentation or meeting) it is useful to do the following:
- State your position clearly
- Structure your argument and link your ideas
- Lead the audience through your logic
- Give reasons to support your argument
- Summarise your argument at the end.

Cultural attitudes may have an impact in this area in the following ways:
- The amount which other people should contribute to the agreement
- The directness of the opinions given and the language used
- The extent to which feelings are shown (see Culture at work).

Task 1

Introduce the topic of the lesson: presenting an argument and giving reasons. Before Ss open their books, write the three kinds of software listed on page 48 on the board as anagrams and see which S can work them out most quickly. Check Ss know what the three software types do. Have Ss ever had problems with viruses or spam at work or at home? Ss discuss why companies should invest in the software listed. Encourage Ss to use the language on page 48 for giving reasons (*due to, in order to* etc.). During feedback, provide further input and practice if necessary (see Language focus below). Also, note on the board key vocabulary which may be useful for the next exercise, e.g. *fraud, hacker, access confidential information, protect data, secure system, security system*.

Suggested answers

Anti-virus software: Because internet virus attacks (which might cause files to become corrupt) are becoming more common.

Firewalls: To act as a barrier between a company's computer network and the outside world (to protect the network from viruses and unauthorised entry).

Spam filters: So that important emails are not lost amongst the large numbers of unwanted advertising emails (spam).

Language focus: Giving reasons

We use the following phrases for giving reasons:

because + verb phrase	*Profits are higher **because** sales have improved.*
because of / due to + noun phrase	*Profits are higher **due to** improved sales.*
due to the fact that + verb phrase	*Profits are higher **due to the fact that** sales have improved.*
the reason ... is + verb phrase	***The reason** profits are higher **is** that sales have improved.*

We use the following phrases for talking about purpose:

to / in order to + infinitive	*We made some staff redundant **in order to** cut overheads.*
so that + verb phrase	*We made staff redundant **so that** we could cut overheads.*

What do you think?

Do Ss know what sort of budget their companies spend on internet security? Explain that they are going to read two proposals arguing for an increase in the budget for internet security. Ss read and decide which proposal makes the case more strongly, then discuss their opinions in pairs. They then report to the rest of the class, giving examples from the texts.

154

UNIT 10

Dervla O'Connor makes the case more strongly because she states her position clearly in the opening sentences, structures her argument, leading the audience through it point by point, and summarises at the end, repeating what she said in the opening section. Fergus Mathews is not as effective because his argument is not structured and includes unnecessary detail (*If I'd had a bigger budget last year…*). Also, it is negative rather than positive (*I can't make the system secure on the budget I've got*). Arguments tend to be effective when they make clear points with some supporting details or examples. The first part of Dervla's argument is quite specific but the second part is a little vague. Perhaps Dervla's argument would be even more persuasive if she added some detail or examples (e.g. the fact that hackers have already been able to access their company database).

Skills book, Good business practice, Presentations, Presenting an effective argument, page 77

What do you say?

Ss are now going to focus on specific language for making a strong case. Ss pick out the phrases Dervla used to structure her argument. Then Ss match the three functions with additional phrases. Give feedback and ensure Ss are comfortable with the pronunciation of the phrases.

1 (That may seem a lot, but) there are two very good reasons why (we need this increase).
2 Firstly …, Secondly …
3 That's why I'm proposing (a substantial increase in the security budget).

1 e   2 b d f   3 c

Skills book, Grammar reference: Linking sentences and ideas, page 95

Listening 1

Ask if Ss think people are interested in brand names. What problems with fakes can arise with brand names? What products are affected by counterfeiting? How can manufacturers prevent it? Focus Ss on the listening scenario. Discuss what the system of electronic identification (ID) tags might consist of. Focus Ss on the first two questions and ask Ss to predict what they think the answers will be. Ss listen to check whether their predictions were correct or not. Play the CD again. This time Ss listen for more detail and also answer Questions 3 and 4.

1 1 c   2 a   3 b
2 a
3 (You may think that . . .) But there are a number of reasons why we need to take action now …
4 That's why I'm proposing (we invest in ID tags).

Listening 2

People who can present an argument strongly not only use a clear structure and linking words, but also use their voice to stress key words. Play the first paragraph of the listening and elicit whether the speaker presents the argument strongly or neutrally. Give feedback. Then divide the class into three groups and allocate one of the speaker's reasons for each group to focus on. As Ss listen, they note the key words that are stressed within their section. Each group then writes their key words on the board. Play the CD again and ask the rest of the class if they agree with the words stressed. Point out that the message can be understood / guessed from these key words, so it is important to choose the correct words to stress (see Language focus below). Then ask Ss to work in pairs, reading out sections of the audioscript, stressing the words in bold. Ss should give their partner feedback. It may also be a good ideas to audio record the Ss for self / peer correction.

1 He presents the argument strongly by stressing key words.
2 See audioscript.

Language focus: Stressing key words

In neutral speech, the key words that are stressed are generally nouns and verbs.
Our **company** has **increased** its **profits** this year.

However, sometimes other words are stressed if we want to emphasise a particular point. The words stressed depend on the speaker's intention.
Our company has **increased** its **profits this** year. (= not *your* company and not *last* year)

Only certain syllables are stressed in multi-syllable words (e.g. *profits*). Ensure Ss know how to use a good learners' dictionary that indicates word stress.

Task 2

Ensure Ss are fairly confident about sentence stress (see Language focus above). Then in pairs Ss decide which words in Dervla's argument on page 49 carry the main message and should therefore be stressed. When Ss have attempted the task themselves, ask them to check their answers on page 99 and to practise reading with the correct sentence stress. Each person

155

should give feedback to their partner. Ss could also record themselves and listen critically. Alternatively, ask one or two Ss to come to the front of the class and present the argument as if they were Dervla; acting it out may emphasise the need to stress key points. (You may need to give a dramatic reading first to provide a model.) Confident Ss may wish to try stressing other words to see how it changes the message.

> **Showing feelings**
> People can become emotional when expressing strong beliefs. However, some cultures express their true emotions more openly than others. This can be overpowering for people who prefer not to reveal their inner thoughts. The opposite can also be true: it can be frustrating to observe someone who appears unaffected by what he / she is saying. We need to remember that the expression of emotions may vary from individual to individual, even within a certain culture. It is also crucial not to assume you are reading another person's feelings correctly, as that could lead to unfortunate misunderstandings.

Culture at work

Ask if Ss tend to become heated and show their feelings when presenting arguments. Or do they stay cool? Do Ss think this is a personal or a cultural issue? Have Ss been in cultures where people behave differently in this respect? If so, how have Ss felt? Refer Ss to the table on page 50. Do Ss have any experience of the situations listed? Where would they put their own culture? Ask Ss to complete their own culture profile about showing feelings on page 82. (Ss identify and mark with a cross where they believe their culture is situated on the line ranging from Show feelings to Stay cool.)

Skills book, Culture profile, page 82

> **Optional activity**
> Before the lesson, find one or several short video clips of people presenting their arguments with emotion. This may involve a person gesticulating, shouting etc. Show the clip and elicit a reaction from Ss. Have they experienced a presentation or meeting like that? What sort of culture would they say the people in the clip are from – people who show their feelings, or who stay cool? (Or would Ss say the appropriate level of emotion to display also depends on the context, e.g. politicians in 'cool' cultures may become very heated when involved in political debate.) Only after this introduction, refer Ss to the table on page 50.

Task 3

Ss now have the chance to bring everything together: to structure an argument, give reasons and stress the key words. Ensure Ss understand the general scenario on page 51.

Step 1: Ss read the three proposals. Check Ss understand by asking a few gist questions. Ss choose one of the proposals each; alternatively, they may prefer to think of their own proposal. Individually, Ss prepare their argument. Encourage them to consider what has been covered in the lesson but discourage them from writing the argument word for word. Refer Ss to the model in the listening activity. Useful phrases are as follows:

So . . . + question
You may think . . . But there are a number of reasons why . . .
The first reason is to . . .
The second reason is to . . .
The third reason is that . . .
That's why I'm proposing that we . . .
Now I'll hand over to X to explain . . .

To promote fluency, Ss make notes only on their arguments, i.e. noting the key words to stress when they speak.

Step 2: Ss present their argument. It may be more effective if Ss stand in front of the class, or in front of smaller sub-groups, to encourage them to present their argument with feeling (rather than sitting in pairs and talking more casually). If time is short, have Ss do Step 1 for homework and present in the following lesson.

Analysis

Allow Ss a few minutes to reflect on the questions individually, then start a group discussion. Give your own feedback. Refer to effective language and any gaps / difficulties.

Self-assessment

Allow Ss a few minutes to think about what they have achieved from the unit and tick the boxes. Suggest what Ss can do to gain further practice.

Video, Part 4

CD-Rom

Unit 11: Negotiate

UNIT OBJECTIVES	
Skills:	Make proposals
	Respond to proposals
	Negotiate a win–win solution
Language:	Gerunds and infinitives
Culture at work:	The importance of relationships

This unit provides an introduction to negotiating. (Ss have the chance of practising negotiating skills further in Unit 15.) When negotiating, it is useful to consider the following:
- Being clear of your own position and proposal
- Explaining the benefits of your proposal
- Establishing your partner's needs and interests
- Being aware of areas you can and cannot concede
- Asking questions to acquire further information if necessary
- Responding to proposals appropriately.

Cultural differences may have an impact on a negotiation in the following ways:
- The amount of time spent on small talk before and after the negotiation
- The directness of the language used in accepting or declining proposals
- The kind of relationship you can expect to have with a negotiating partner (see Culture at work).

Skills book, Unit 15, page 70

Teacher's book, page 171

Task 1

Introduce the topic of the lesson: negotiating. Ask Ss what experience they have of negotiating, and to give examples of negotiations they have taken part in. Point out that everyone negotiates, whether it is a pay rise, a business deal, when to take leave, where to go on holiday, who should do the washing up etc. One stage of negotiating involves making proposals and responding to them. Refer Ss to the list of useful phrases and ask for one or two examples, writing them on the board. Ensure that Ss are confident about the grammatical constructions used after the various phrases (see Language focus below). Ask Ss to read Task 1 and ensure that they understand what they have to do and that there is a strict time limit. (It is important to keep to this.) Also ensure

Ss do not look at the possible solutions on page 104 before you tell them to do so. In pairs Ss negotiate a deal. Monitor and give feedback. Then refer to the possible solutions on page 104. What do Ss think of these suggestions?

Language focus: Use of the gerund in proposals

We use the gerund after prepositions.
*What **about** / How **about giving** me the complete amount?*

We also use the gerund after certain verbs.
*We could **consider giving** it to charity.
I **suggest investing** the money.*

Note that *suggest* is never followed by *to*.

Analysis, Task 1

Allow Ss to reflect individually then open up a group discussion. One of the key issues is that more than one solution is possible. In any negotiation, it is unadvisable to fix on one position or solution only (e.g. 60:40 in my favour). If both parties were stubborn and refused to move from their original position, it would be impossible to reach agreement (and in this activity, the time limit would run out). Instead, it makes sense to think creatively about finding a solution. The starting point for this is to break your position down into a number of objectives that you want to achieve. It then becomes possible to realise that you may be able to meet your objectives in a number of ways.

Skills book, Possible solutions, page 104

What do you think? 1

Ss now think about strategies for negotiating. In pairs Ss discuss the questions. Point out that the language used when negotiating depends on your view of the negotiation. If you feel that there are many ways that both parties can reach a win–win agreement, the language used will be quite open and exploratory. On the other hand, if you favour a win–lose approach, the language used is likely to be much more direct.

The win–win approach is generally considered the best approach to negotiation as both parties then achieve some or most of their aims. Of course, a win–win approach is not appropriate in every situation, e.g. if the parties are clearly making a short-term deal only. Also, if one party is in a position of greater power, the deal may not be a true negotiation and win–win is irrelevant.

What do you think? 2

Ask Ss to work in pairs and decide which strategies are useful for finding a win–win solution. Then discuss the strategies together, with Ss giving reasons for their views.

> All of the strategies are good for finding a win–win solution **except** for the following:
>
> - ~~If you don't agree, say 'no'.~~ It is important not to be bullied into accepting a 'lose' solution. However, it can be more productive to say something neutral, e.g. *I think I can understand your position*, and then to ask questions which allow you to understand the other party's needs.
>
> - ~~Keep repeating your demands.~~ If the other party has declined your proposal, it may not meet their needs. So instead of focusing on your position, seek instead a way of finding a proposal that will meet some of their interests and needs.

Skills book, Good business practice, Negotiating, Negotiation strategies, page 81

Listening

Explain that Ss are going to listen to two negotiations. In the first negotiation Viktor, a supplier, is talking to Xavier; in the second he is talking to Yacoub. Ensure Ss understand the situation. Ask Ss to listen and think about the answer to Question 1 only. Ss listen to both negotiations and answer the question. Discuss Ss's answers, asking for reasons. Ss are now going to focus on the language used in the negotiations. Ask them to look at Question 2 and to listen to the first negotiation again. Elicit Ss' answers. Then ask Ss to look at Questions 3 and 4 and to listen to the second negotiation again. Elicit Ss' answers.

> 1 The buyer in the second negotiation (Yacoub) is more likely to reach an agreement. In the first agreement Xavier simply says no to the proposal instead of seeking to find a solution that might meet some of Viktor's interests. In the second negotiation, on the other hand, Yacoub makes a proposal that might meet Viktor's needs without Yacoub losing anything.
>
> 2 Xavier refuses to accept what Viktor is saying: *It's totally unacceptable. We'll have to switch to another supplier if you insist on this.*
>
> 3 Yacoub says that he sees Viktor's position. He asks for further details and then make another proposal. He also points out the benefits of the new proposal: *I see. Well, I can understand your position. But how much are you thinking of charging? Here's another idea. How about a flat rate of – say 20 euros per delivery? That way, we could save money by ... And you'd gain because you wouldn't have to deliver so often. And you could ..., which would be much more economical.*
>
> 4 He expresses interest but does not commit himself: *Well, it sounds like a reasonable idea ... But I'll need to do some calculations to see how it would work.*

Culture at work

Ss close their books. Draw the outline of the Culture at work table from page 53 on the board with top and left headings. Explain that you are going to say some features of long and short-term relationships; you would like Ss to decide if each feature refers to the long term or short term and where to write it in the table. Then read, in random order, sentences from the table on page 53. Ss tell you where in the table to write notes on it. Do Ss have any experience of the situations listed? Where would they put their own culture? How do they feel when interacting with people from the other type of culture? Ask Ss to complete their own culture profile about the importance of relationships on page 82.

Skills book, Culture profile, page 82

> **Optional activity**
> Instead of doing the Culture at work activity as above, prepare one set of cards before the lesson containing each of the ideas from the table on page 53. Ss attach the cards to the appropriate cell in the table on the board using magnets or sticking tape. Ss check their answers by looking at the table on page 53.

What do you say? 1

Elicit answers to the question about responding to proposals you do not want to accept. If necessary, refer Ss back to the listening activity. Xavier in the first negotiation rejected the proposal, refusing to consider it, resulting in the end of their business relationship. Yacoub, on the other hand, asked questions to find out what Viktor's interests were and then suggested a proposal in both their interests.

Refer Ss to the strategies used in the listening activity. Specific phrases are shown in the next exercise.

What do you say? 2

Ss match specific phrases from the listening with the strategies for responding to proposals. In feedback, ensure Ss are comfortable with the pronunciation of the phrases. Review the use of the gerund in negotiating phrases in general terms. See Language focus on page 172.

UNIT 11

1 b 2 c 3 h 4 g 5 d 6 e 7 f 8 g 9 d 10 a

> **Optional activity**
> **Photocopiable resource 11.1 (page 181)**
> Take this opportunity to review the use of gerunds and infinitives in general by doing a card sort. Ss work in pairs. Photocopy and distribute the cards. Ask Ss to group them under the appropriate heading: gerund or infinitive. Ask Ss to look at the Grammar reference on page 96 to check their answers. Then deal with any questions Ss may have.
>
> **Answers**
> **Gerund:** before, after, without, look forward to, it's no good, consider, postpone, risk, suggest, avoid, advise, recommend, how about
> **Infinitive:** it's easy, it's important, agree, aim, decide, afford, promise
> **Both:** like, prefer, remember

📑 Skills book, Grammar reference: Gerunds and infinitives, page 96

Task 2

Ss now have a chance to prepare and practise responding to proposals. Point out to Ss that thinking about appropriate strategies is the first stage; the second stage is to think of the appropriate language to express them in. Ensure Ss understand the two situations.

Step 1: Divide the class into pairs: A and B. Ss individually prepare proposals for each situation. They should also predict what proposals their partner might make and prepare responses to these proposals. It is desirable to generate a number of possible solutions.

Step 2: Ss role play the scenarios, using the strategies and language they have prepared. Monitor Ss' performance.

> **Possible solutions**
>
> **Situation 1:** B goes to the party and starts work early the next day, B goes to the party and works extra another time, everyone starts early on Saturday and finishes at 3
>
> **Situation 2:** Set up a system of flexible benefits with core holiday of 25 or 30 days plus additional benefits (which may be pay, holiday or other benefits), Organise a vote among the staff of the two companies, Offer extra holiday as a reward for long service and good performance

Analysis, Task 2

Allow Ss a few minutes to reflect on the questions individually, then start a group discussion. Give your own feedback.

Task 3

Step 1: Ss now have the chance to bring everything together: to make proposals, respond to proposals and to negotiate a win–win solution. Divide the class into pairs: A and B. Ensure Ss understand the background to the situation.

Step 2: Refer Ss to their roles on page 99 and page 102 and encourage them to think of their objectives in the negotiation: what must they achieve and what would it be good to achieve? Also, what could they concede and what is it impossible to concede? Encourage Ss not to think of one solution only but of the separate elements within a solution. (If Ss have identified the separate elements, these can be repackaged into different solutions.) It may help if all Ss playing role A prepare together, and all Ss playing role B prepare together. Move around the class offering help as required. In pairs, Ss negotiate, aiming for a win–win solution. Monitor and take notes. You may wish to audio or video record the roleplays for T feedback and self / peer feedback later.

Analysis, Task 3

Allow Ss a few minutes to reflect on the questions individually, then start a group discussion. Give your own feedback.

Self-assessment

Allow Ss a few minutes to think about what they have achieved from the unit and tick the boxes. Suggest what Ss can do to gain further practice.

📑 Teacher's book, Negotiation planner, page 184
📑 Video, Part 4
📑 CD-Rom

159

INTELLIGENT BUSINESS (INTERMEDIATE) TEACHER'S BOOK: SKILLS BOOK

Unit 12: Participate in meetings

UNIT OBJECTIVES	
Skills:	Put your point of view
Listen and take turns
Make your case and respond
Language:	Modal verbs (*must, should, need, have to, could*)
Culture at work:	Attitudes to silence during discussions

When participating in meetings, it is useful to consider the following:
- The importance of the agenda
- The role of the chairperson or leader
- Making a point effectively and persuading others
- Active listening
- Asking for and giving clarification
- Turn-taking
- Record-keeping and minute-taking.

Cultural attitudes may affect:
- How a meeting is organised and run
- How often meetings are held and how long they last
- How central a role the chairperson plays
- How much participants are expected to contribute
- The extent to which turn-taking happens
- The extent to which silence and interruptions are tolerated (see Culture at work).

Task 1

Start the lesson with Ss' books closed. Introduce the topic of the lesson: participating in meetings. Write the viewpoint from Task 1 on the board. Ask Ss for their reactions. After the discussion, ask Ss to open their books and compare the language they used with the list of phrases on page 56. Point out it is not enough simply to state your own opinion; it is more effective to try to persuade others to change their views. This is why questioning is useful in meetings:

Don't you think that ...?
Wouldn't you agree that ...?

Analysis, Task 1

Allow Ss to reflect individually then open up a group discussion.

What do you think?

Ss now think about how meetings can be made effective (rather than a waste of time). Refer Ss to the *Before the meeting* and *During the meeting* lists on page 57 and check comprehension. In pairs, Ss tick the points they both agree with. Ss may want to make notes on those points they disagree on. Open up to a group discussion.

Suggested answers
The points which help make meetings more effective are:
Read the minutes of the previous meeting.
Make only relevant and interesting points.
Make sure everyone understands your point of view.
Listen carefully to other people's points of view.
Find out what different people think.
Try to reach a conclusion that everyone can feel satisfied with.

Skills book, Good business practice, Meetings, Participating in meetings, page 78

What do you say?

It will be clear from the previous activity that participants in a meeting need to listen carefully, respond and take turns (rather than dominating). This activity focuses on responding and turn-taking. Ss match each function with a phrase. Check Ss' answers then elicit any other phrases Ss may know for each function. Write them on the board and practise their pronunciation.

1 d   2 e   3 c   4 a   5 f   6 b

Other possible phrases to match the functions
1 Yes – and I think we should also remember that ...
   I agree – and what's more, ...
2 Perhaps ... is something we also need to consider
   On the other hand, it might be better to ...
3 I'm afraid that's not quite what I meant
   Actually that's not quite right
4 I'd just like to say that ...
   Can I just point out that ...
   Sorry to interrupt but ...
5 Let me just finish what I'm saying
   Just let me finish – I was going to say that ...
6 Another argument is ...
   And another thing is that...

160

Listening 1

Explain that Ss are going to listen to extracts from a meeting. Ask Ss if the general public in their countries are aware of what they eat from a health point of view. Ask if Ss have noticed any changes in what food manufacturers are producing as a result of greater public awareness of health issues. Set the scene for the listening. Play the listening the first time, all the way through, and ask Ss to listen globally and note what the participants are discussing in each extract. Then, listening a second time, Ss write the number of the extract next to each function on page 58.

a 2   b 1   c 5   d 4   e 6   f 3

Listening 2

Let Ss listen a third time to note down the exact phrases used for each function. Or ask Ss to turn to the audioscript on pages 110–111 and underline the phrases. In feedback, check that Ss are comfortable with the pronunciation of the phrases.

a I agree. And what's more, …
b On the other hand, it might be better to …
c Actually, that's not quite right.
d Sorry to interrupt, but can I just ask …?
e Just let me finish. I was going to say that …
f Can I just point out that …

Task 2

Ss now have the chance to use some of the functions from the previous activities. Before starting the task, briefly remind Ss not to overuse *should* for making suggestions; other modal verbs such as *could* are also useful (see Language focus below). Divide the class into small groups (3–4 Ss per group) and refer Ss to the topics and the framework. Check comprehension. (For larger groups, possibly ask one subgroup to demonstrate how the framework works in front of the whole class.) Encourage each role to develop their point before the next person cuts in. Monitor Ss's performance.

Analysis, Task 2

Allow Ss a few minutes to reflect on the questions individually, then start a group discussion. Give your own feedback. Refer to effective language and any gaps / difficulties.

Skills book, Grammar reference: Modal verbs, part 2, page 88

Language focus: Use of *could* in suggestions

We often use *should* when making suggestions.
*I think we **should** make the change now.*

It is equally common to use *could* for suggestions.
***Perhaps** we **could** wait and see if there really is demand for the product.*
***Couldn't** we do some research before taking action?*

We also use *could* for talking about the consequences of a suggestion.
*It **could** destroy us if we had to fight a lawsuit like that.*

Culture at work

Ss have their books closed. Write the following on the board or on cards to use as prompts: *Silence, Interruptions, Turn-taking*. Elicit reactions from the Ss about the three areas in the context of meetings. If you have a multinational group, there should be some interesting differences. Refer Ss to the Culture at work box on page 59. Elicit any additional reactions to the information. Do Ss feel that their cultural style matches the description given? Then ask Ss to complete their own culture profile about attitudes to silence on page 82. (Ss identify and mark with a cross where they believe their culture is situated on the line ranging from Anglo-Saxon to Asian.)

Skills book, Culture profile, page 82

Optional activity
An alternative way in to the topic of attitudes to silence is to think of discussion and silence in visual terms. Draw the following on the board: __ __ __ __
Do Ss think it represents the speech of Anglo-Saxon, Latin or Asian cultures? The answer is Anglo-Saxon. Latin cutures can be represented by overlapping lines. Asian cultures can be shown by bigger gaps between the lines.

Task 3

If possible, before the lesson, collect pictures of food mixers, juice extractors and toasters to use to check comprehension when setting the scene for Task 3. Refer Ss to page 59 and explain they that now have the chance to bring everything together in a meeting role-play. Check that Ss understand the scenario. Ss work in groups of four. Ask Ss to choose a role from the list on page 59; weaker Ss should be given the chance to choose first. Ss then turn to the roles in the back of the book to prepare their thoughts. Help any Ss who need input while preparing their role. Encourage Ss to write notes only rather than a full script. Also encourage Ss to think of their overall objectives while they are planning, not just the detail, e.g. if they think (and can get other participants to agree) that the company needs to save money to survive, then they must all work together to find a solution which achieves that. Ss start the meeting when they are ready. Monitor the discussion and take notes for use during feedback. You may wish to audio or video record the role-play to enable self / peer correction.

Analysis, Task 3

Allow Ss a few minutes to reflect on the questions individually, then start a group discussion. Give your own feedback. Refer to effective language and any gaps / difficulties.

Self-assessment

Allow Ss a few minutes to think about what they have achieved from the unit and tick the boxes. Suggest what Ss can do to gain further practice.

Video, Part 4

CD-Rom

Writing 4: Formal correspondence

UNIT OBJECTIVES	
Skills:	Reply to an enquiry
	Apologise and give reasons
Language:	Gerunds and infinitives

The following may be important when writing formal letters or emails:
- The reader (What is their relationship to the writer? What is their level of knowledge of the subject and their level of English?)
- The purpose of the correspondence
- The structure of the letter or email
- Clarity, conciseness, consistency
- The level of formality
- Tone
- Accuracy (grammar, spelling, punctuation).

Cultural attitudes may have an impact on the following:
- Formality of language
- Use of titles in the greeting
- Tone (e.g. in requests).

- Style guide, Letters, page 16
- Style guide, Emails, page 18
- Style guide, Faxes, page 20
- Style guide, General rules, page 3
- Style guide, Organising your writing, page 4
- Teacher's book, Writing preparation framework, page 188
- Teacher's book, Writing feedback framework, page 189
- Teacher's book, page 142

Introduce the topic of the session: writing formal correspondence (letters / faxes / emails). Ask Ss what kind of formal correspondence they write and / or read. Point out that the same issues apply to all types of correspondence; whether a document is sent by post, fax or email often does not change the way it is written. Emails can be as formal as letters and therefore cannot always be written quickly. Write three headings on the board (*Structure, Vocabulary, Grammar*) and elicit what contributes towards an email or letter being considered formal. (See Language focus sections below and on page 142.) The first exercise focuses particularly on structure. Ss match each section of the letter with a description. Check Ss' answers then focus on the language used in the letter. Encourage Ss to suggest alternative possible phrases for each section. Also draw Ss' attention to the use of the present simple in *I enclose…* and *I look forward to…* (which creates a more formal impression than the simple form).

a 4   b 1   c 7   d 8   e 2   f 5   g 6   h 3

Language focus: Formal correspondence

The following is typical of the structure of formal correspondence.

Subject line	*Proposal for IT maintenance contract* (before or after formal greeting)
Formal greeting	*Dear Mr Black*
Reference to previous contact	*Thank you for your letter of 5 June.* *I refer to your telephone call of 10 July.* *Further to our discussion, I am writing to …*
Offer to be helpful	*Please let me know if you have any questions.* *Please do not hesitate to contact me if you have any questions.* *Please do contact me if you would like any further information.*
Reference to future contact	*I look forward to hearing from you.* *I look forward to your reply.*
Formal ending	*Yours sincerely*

See the section on formal vocabulary and grammar in Writing 2 of the Teacher's book (page 142).

Language focus: Greetings and endings

Greeting	Ending	
Dear Mr Jones *Dear Ms Jones*	*Yours sincerely*	The recipient's name is known. *Dear Miss …* is uncommon today. If a woman's marital status is not known, use *Dear Ms …,*
Dear Sir *Dear Madam* *Dear Sirs*	*Yours faithfully*	The recipient's name is not known
Dear Alex	*Regards* *Best regards* *Best wishes*	The writer knows the recipient quite well

Note that some cultures place a great deal of importance on academic titles, e.g. *Dear Dr Barker.*

163

INTELLIGENT BUSINESS (INTERMEDIATE) TEACHER'S BOOK: SKILLS BOOK WRITING 4

Task 1

Explain that Ss will now write a formal letter using the same structure as in the previous activity. Ss read the letter on the bottom left of the page and answer the following questions: *Who wrote the letter? What is he interested in? What specifically does he want? How does he expect to receive it?* Then point Ss to the notes on the right, which they should incorporate into their reply. Ss write a formal letter. Encourage peer correction before giving your feedback.

Suggested answer
Dear Mr Bradshaw
Your enquiry regarding IT training courses
I refer to your letter of 15 July expressing interest in our courses. Please find enclosed our programme for this year. May I take this opportunity to explain a little about our company? A-1 Training is an established training company with 30 years' experience of training IT professionals in the latest technology. We would be happy to offer advice on selecting the appropriate course for you from the wide range we offer.
Please do contact me if you would like any further information about the courses. My direct telephone number is 02076234444.
I look forward to hearing from you.
Yours sincerely

What do you write?

Elicit possible reasons for writing letters (e.g. to place an order, complain, apologise, give information, give news, confirm plans, express thanks). Then elicit specific reasons for writing a letter of apology (late delivery, goods out of stock, poor service etc.). Explain that Ss are going to see a jumbled email about problems with a delivery. Elicit why there might be problems and write key vocabulary on the board, e.g. *high demand, supplies, out of stock, dispatch an order*. Ss then look at the jumbled email and reorder the phrases. You may wish to ask Ss to work in pairs or small groups, especially if Ss are weaker. Give feedback and draw attention to the language used in the email. You may wish to take this opportunity to review briefly the uses of gerunds and infinitives relevant to correspondence. (See Optional activity below.)

1 Dear Ms Bundy
2 Thank you for your order dated March 30.
3 We have items A24 and B39 in stock **4** and you should receive them in 2–3 days. **5** We regret that we are out of stock of item C21 **6** due to a high demand for this product at the present time. **7** We hope to receive new supplies within the next 7–10 days. **8** We will dispatch your order as soon as possible after that. **9** We apologise for any inconvenience this may cause.
10 Yours sincerely

Optional activity
Write the following sentences from the letter to Ms Bundy on the board:
We hope to receive new supplies within … .
We apologise for any inconvenience this may cause.
Thank you for your order dated March 30.

Ask Ss to think of as many alternative endings as possible for the underlined phrases. Review gerunds and infinitives. (See Language focus below and the Grammar reference on page 96.)

Language focus:
Use of gerunds after prepositions

Prepositions can be followed by a noun or *-ing*.

I apologise for   any inconvenience caused.
             causing any inconvenience.

To is usually followed by the infinitive However, sometimes *to* is used as a preposition.

I look forward to   your reply / receiving your reply.

Skills book, Grammar reference, Gerunds and infinitives, page 96

Task 2

Ss are now going to write a formal letter. They should aim to structure their letter suitably, and use appropriate and accurate language. Ss show each other their writing for peer correction. If computers and a projector are available, Ss should type their memo using a computer. Alternatively, ask Ss to write the letter for homework. Give your feedback.

Suggested answer
Dear Mr X
Building Customer Confidence
Thank you for enquiring about our workshop on Building Customer Confidence on 6 June.
I regret that we are unable to offer you a place due to high demand for the course. The maximum number of participants (35) has already enrolled on the course. However, because of the popularity of the course, we plan to hold a repeat session later in the year and will inform you of the new date as soon as it is fixed.
In the meantime, we apologise for any inconvenience this may cause. Should any cancellations arise for the workshop on 6 June, we will inform you as soon as possible.
Yours sincerely

Unit 13: Lead a meeting

UNIT OBJECTIVES	
Skills:	Summarise main points
	Encourage people to speak
	Control the meeting
Language:	Reported speech
Culture at work:	Attitudes to interruptions

Unit 12 focused on skills used when participating in meetings. This unit builds on those skills. When leading meetings, it is useful to consider the following:
- Controlling the meeting in terms of keeping to the scheduled time and ensuring the desired outcome is achieved
- Ensuring the discussion follows the agenda and digressions are avoided
- Encouraging participants to contribute to the discussion and keeping potentially dominant speakers under control
- Clarifying any unclear issues
- Summarising the main points.

Cultural attitudes (relating to both national and organisational culture) may have an impact on:
- The role the chairperson / leader plays and the reaction of the other participants to that person
- The pre-meeting organisation, e.g. the circulation of a written agenda
- The structure and formality of the meeting
- Punctuality within meetings, and length of and frequency of meetings
- The post-meeting follow-up, including circulation of written minutes
- The amount of socialising / small talk around the meeting.

Some of the above items may also be affected by the type of meeting, e.g. board meeting, AGM, departmental meeting, team update.

What do you think?

Ss start the lesson with their books closed. Draw on the board a spider diagram with *meeting* at the centre. Write the verb *organise* at the end of one line coming from the centre and elicit further verbs that collocate with *meeting* (e.g. *have a meeting, hold a meeting, run a meeting, lead a meeting, chair a meeting, attend a meeting, cancel a meeting, postpone a meeting, bring forward a meeting*). Explain that the topic of the lesson is leading a meeting. Ask Ss if they think there are any differences between leading a meeting and chairing a meeting. They are basically the same thing; however, if the verb *chair* is used, the meeting is likely to be run more formally.)

Now draw on the board another spider diagram or mind map, with *Leading a meeting* in the centre. Ask Ss to work in small groups and brainstorm ideas as to what this involves. If possible, give each group a large piece of paper (e.g. a flipchart sheet) to note their ideas on in the form of a spider diagram or mind map. One member of the group should note down the ideas and be prepared to report back.

Suggested answers
An effective leader of a meeting:
- makes the objectives and procedure of the meeting clear at the beginning
- ensures that everyone has a chance to contribute
- asks speakers to give further information if necessary
- clarifies anything that is not clear
- ensures that speakers stay on track
- does not allow any one person to dominate at the expense of others
- summarises key points and action to be taken.

Task 1

Before asking Ss to report back, ask them to open their books and look at the phrases on page 62. Then ask one member of each group to report back to the rest of the class, sharing the ideas that they noted down.

Analysis, Task 1

Allow Ss to reflect individually then open up a group discussion. Link discussion of the role of a leader of a meeting with a focus on the skill of summarising. The leader of a meeting often nominates someone to take minutes and to report what has been said. However, the leader often has to summarise issues throughout the meeting; he / she also usually summarises key points at the end of the meeting and action to be taken. Explain that when we are reporting what has been said, we are usually interested in the overall meaning rather than the specific words that have been said.

INTELLIGENT BUSINESS (INTERMEDIATE) TEACHER'S BOOK: SKILLS BOOK

Optional activity
Photocopiable resource 13.1 (page 182)
Do this activity if you feel Ss need more help with summarising and reported speech. Ss work in pairs. Photocopy and distribute a set of cards to each pair. Ss match pairs of cards (direct speech and a report of what was said). Check Ss' answers. Focus on the reporting verbs used, elicit any others and, if necessary, practise the grammatical structures. (See Grammar reference on page 97.)

Skills book, Grammar reference: Reported speech, page 97

Skills book, Good business practice, Meetings, Leading a meeting, page 79

Listening

Explain that Ss are going to listen to extracts from a meeting about where to hold the next sales team meeting. They are going to focus on what the leader does in each extract. Ask Ss to predict a possible order for the actions on page 63 and to suggest the language that the leader might use. Ss then listen and write the number of the extract next to each action. Check Ss' answers and discuss the language used for each action.

a 5   b 4   c 2   d 6   e 1   f 3

What do you say?

Ss now have the chance to focus on language for leading a meeting. Referring back to the list in the Listening exercise, Ss match the phrases. Elicit any additional phrases that Ss know for each function. Practise the pronunciation of the phrases if required.

1 f   2 c   3 e   4 d   5 a   6 b

Other possible phrases to match the functions
a That's not part of today's agenda, I think we're getting sidetracked
b So, am I correct in thinking you mean …?
c Go on, Could you expand on that?
d Right then, to summarise, …
e Margaret, would you like to say something here?
f Joakim, could you let Paola say something?

Task 2

Ss now have the chance to practise leading a mini-meeting, using some of the functional language from the previous activities. Divide the class into small groups and refer Ss to the topics. Check comprehension. Alternatively, you may wish to suggest other, more relevant topics for pre-experience Ss. Ss then hold mini-meetings, taking it in turn to be leader. If time is short, those who summarised in Task 1 need not do it again here. Some Ss will also get a chance to be leaders in Task 3. If equipment is available, you may want to audio or video record for self / peer correction. Otherwise, take notes yourself in preparation for the feedback session.

Optional activity
Photocopiable resource 13.2 (page 182)
In order to encourage the meeting leader to practise the range of skills required, give role cards to the participants. Ss work in groups of no more than five. Photocopy and give a card to each participant in the mini meetings in Task 2. The meeting participants should do as the card says and the meeting leader should respond appropriately. Monitor the mini-meetings and give feedback.

Culture at work

Ask Ss whether they have experience of attending or leading meetings in different countries and cultures. If so, ask what they experienced in terms of punctuality, agenda and organisation? If Ss do not have any experience, ask for their ideas on how attitudes to these three areas could vary. Refer Ss to the table on page 64 and elicit any additional reactions to the information. Then ask Ss to complete their own culture profile about attitudes to interruptions on page 82. (Ss identify and mark with a cross where they believe their culture is situated on the line ranging from One task at a time to Several tasks at once. You may wish to ask Ss to write two marks on the line: a cross indicating their company culture, and a circle indicating the culture in general in their country.)

Skills book, Culture profile, page 82

Optional activity
By now, you will have established how meetings are run in the Ss' countries. You might want to focus on what this means in terms of specific language. Ask Ss what their reaction would be if they were chairing / leading a meeting in each of the following scenarios. What would they say?

1 You are halfway through a meeting and a participant arrives late. What do you say?
2 A participant has started to discuss a point which is not on the agenda. What do you say?
3 A participant's mobile phone rings during the meeting and he excuses himself in order to take the call. What do you say?
4 One of the participants has a tendency to dominate. She has just started speaking and you notice other participants looking unhappy. What do you say?
5 Discussion about one agenda item has led into discussion of three agenda items. What do you say?

Task 3

Explain that Ss are now going to take part in mini-meetings in which they will express their own views (rather than follow given roles). Refer Ss to the situations on page 65 (alternatively you, or the Ss, could suggest other topics) and appoint a leader for each situation. Ensure that all Ss have had a chance to lead a meeting by the end of the lesson. Instead of doing all four scenarios, you may prefer to focus on a few scenarios only, allowing Ss to spend longer on them. Monitor the mini-meetings and take notes for use during feedback. You may wish to audio or video record the meetings to enable self / peer correction.

Analysis

Allow Ss a few minutes to reflect on the questions individually, then start a group discussion. Give your own feedback. Refer to effective language and any gaps / difficulties.

Self-assessment

Allow Ss a few minutes to think about what they have achieved from the unit and tick the boxes. Suggest what Ss can do to gain further practice.

- Video, Part 5
- CD-Rom

INTELLIGENT BUSINESS (INTERMEDIATE) TEACHER'S BOOK: SKILLS BOOK

Unit 14: Conclude a presentation

UNIT OBJECTIVES	
Skills:	Make a strong conclusion
	Ask questions
	Deal with questions
Language:	Questions
Culture at work:	Attitudes to critical questions

Units 3, 6 and 8 looked at skills needed when giving a presentation. This unit builds on those skills. (Units 3, 8 and 14 of the Coursebook also focus on presentations.) When concluding a presentation, it is useful to consider the following:
- Summarising the main points
- Finishing on a strong note and a good final sentence
- Thanking the audience for their attention
- Inviting questions if they have not been asked during the presentation
- Dealing with questions effectively.

Cultural attitudes may affect:
- whether questions are asked, and at what stage
- the way in which questions are formulated (direct vs. less direct)
- the kind of answer given (direct vs. vague response).

What do you think?

Start the lesson with Ss' books closed. Introduce the topic of the lesson: concluding a presentation. Ask Ss what they think makes a strong end to a presentation. Collate ideas on the board and elicit a sample phrase for each strategy. Then refer Ss to the list of strategies and phrases on page 66. Ss match the tips on ending a presentation with the appropriate phrases. In pairs Ss decide which are effective ways of ending a presentation. Elicit the answers and give feedback.

1 d 2 f 3 a 4 e 5 b 6 g 7 c 8 h

Skills book, Good business practice, Presentations, Ending a presentation, page 77

Listening 1

Explain that Ss are going to listen to the last part of a presentation. Introduce the situation on page 66 about whether to outsource distribution or build a warehouse. Ask Ss to listen for gist as they listen for the first time (without looking at the questions on page 66). Which option does the speaker propose and why? (The speaker proposes that the company builds its own warehouse in order to save money and enable more efficient deliveries.) Then refer Ss to the questions on page 66. Play the CD again and Ss answer the questions. You may need to play the CD several times, or stop after the relevant section to allow Ss to write the phrases used. Note that some of the phrases that Ss should write down are the same as in the previous exercise. Give Ss feedback on their answers. Elicit any other phrases Ss can think of to conclude a presentation. Ensure that Ss can pronounce the phrases correctly as they will need them in Task 1. The *Good business practice* section suggests that Ss should prepare the final sentence of a talk beforehand – so focus on the pronunciation of the final sentence. (See Language focus below.) Point out that the stressed words in the final sentence are in bold in the audioscript.

1 The steps included in the listening are:
   Summarise the main points (6)
   Make a strong final statement (2)
   Thank the audience for listening (4)
   Ask for questions (3)
2 a So to sum up
   b We've looked at two main points
   c As we have seen
3 a The main conclusion is that the new warehouse should be built as soon as possible
   b My conclusion is, therefore, that …
   c The final sentence of the body of the presentation begins: Then we can have the benefits of …

Language focus: Ending a presentation

It is important to end a presentation strongly. This can be done by stressing the key words in the final sentence of the body of the presentation.
*Then we can have the benefits of greater **cost savings** and greater **efficiency** in the **future**.*

It is also important to ensure that your intonation falls strongly to signal the end. (Otherwise, the audience may be unsure whether the presentation has finished.) In the following example, the final stress is on the middle syllable of *attention*; the intonation should drop sharply following this final stressed syllable.
*Thank you for your **attention**.*

168

UNIT 14

Task 1

Ss will now practise ending a presentation. Refer Ss to the situation on page 67 and to the table showing information about the two potential warehouse sites. Ensure Ss understand (e.g. *brownfield* vs. *greenfield*).

Step 1: Divide the class into pairs, A and B. Ss read the role information carefully and prepare their summary and conclusion individually. Monitor and help as necessary.

Step 2: In their pairs, Ss present their case to their partner. You may also want one or two Ss to present to the whole class.

> **Suggested answer (Site A)**
> So to sum up ...
> We've compared Site A and Site B, looking at four main areas: the type of site (brownfield or greenfield), road access, proximity to the factory, and the cost of land. As we've seen, Site A is only three kilometres from the factory (as opposed to 35 kilometres for Site B); and it will cost only €500,000 (€300,000 less than Site B). My conclusion is, therefore, that we select Site A. Then we can have the benefits of lower cost and closer proximity to the factory. I think that's all I have to say. Thank you for your attention ... Any questions?
> (The same structure could be used for Site B; the facts would need to be changed.)

Analysis, Task 1

Allow Ss to reflect individually then open up a group discussion. Provide a model if you think it would be useful.

Listening 2

Ss now have the chance to consider strategies for asking and dealing with questions at the end of a presentation. Explain that Ss will hear the question and answer session following the end of the presentation in Listening 1. Can Ss predict any questions that might be asked? Ss listen globally to see if they were correct. Then refer Ss to the questions on page 67 and Ss listen again, this time in more detail. You may need to play the CD several times, especially to allow Ss to note down what is said. Give feedback on Ss' answers.

> 1 The four questions are:
> **Question 1:** Building a warehouse is a big investment. Can you please explain how we're going to manage it?
> **Question 2:** Surely it's too risky. What if there's a drop in sales?
> **Question 3:** So what are the sales projections for the next five years?
> **Question 4:** You say that the cost of maintaining a warehouse would be low. Can you give us a full breakdown of running costs please?

> 2 **a** 3 **b** 1 **c** 2 **d** 4
>
> 3 The presenter deals with the problems in the following ways:
> **Problem a:** The presenter cannot answer now but offers to find out the information (I'm afraid I don't have that information here, but I can find out for you)
> **Problem b:** The presenter asks for clarification (Sorry – are you asking about financing?)
> **Problem c:** The presenter accepts the validity of the question before responding (That's a good question. But …)
> **Problem d:** The presenter says he will deal with the question at another time (Sorry, I don't think we have time to go into that now, but we'll be discussing the details at our next meeting)

> **Language focus:**
> **Questions following a presentation**
>
> Effective questions following a presentation are often split into two stages and are usually linked directly to what the presenter said. There are a number of ways of linking back to the presentation:
>
> **Quotation from the presentation + question**
> *You say that the cost of maintaining a warehouse would be low. Can you give us a full breakdown of costs?*
>
> **Comment about what was said in the presentation + question**
> *Building a warehouse is a big investment. Can you please explain how we're going to manage it?*
>
> *So* **+ question**
> *So what are the sales projections for the next five years?*
>
> It is also common to split questions into two stages even when not referring directly to the presentation.
>
> **Polite (indirect) general question + specific question**
> *Would you mind telling us a bit about the financing of this project? Where exactly is the money coming from?*

Task 2

Before starting Task 2, ensure Ss feel confident about asking questions. See the Grammar reference on page 86 for a reminder on the formation of questions if necessary. Also refer to the practice of asking two-stage questions following a presentation (see Language focus above.)

Step 1: Divide the class into pairs or small groups so that As from Task 1 are working together, as are Bs. Ss prepare questions as a follow-up to the other person's presentation

169

conclusion from Task 1. Ss prepare six questions based on the points listed on page 68. You may want to brainstorm some ideas with the class as a whole first. Remind Ss to refer back to the speaker's presentation when asking questions so that the relevance of the questions is clear.

Step 2: Ss compare their prepared questions with other Ss. Ask Ss to read to the rest of the class their most challenging questions. Ss will have the opportunity to ask and get a response to their questions in Task 3.

> **Suggested answers**
> 1 Do you mind if I ask about recruitment? How easy will it be to find appropriately skilled employees to work at Site A?
> 2 In your presentation, you proposed that we select Site A, the brownfield site previously occupied by a chemical plant. Surely the site will suffer from environmental problems. Can you clarify this and explain how you plan to deal with any such problems?
> 3 So what are the company's plans for providing adequate security?
> 4 I don't think the plan is for our company to occupy the whole industrial zone. Do you know if the government has any plans for other development in the area?
> 5 You said that Site A is only three kilometres from our factory. Does this mean that transport costs will be lower than for site B (bearing in mind that Site B has easy access to the motorway network)?
> 6 You made the point that the cost of land is €300,000 lower for Site A than for Site B. What about other costs associated with the site?

> **Optional activity**
> **Photocopiable resource 14.1 (page 183)**
> To provide more practice on asking two-part questions, photocopy and distribute to each S the worksheet on page 183. Ss produce questions that could be asked at the end of a presentation, using the prompts. Ss may work in pairs or small groups if they prefer. Elicit a few examples first to ensure Ss understand the task. Monitor and give feedback.

Skills book, Grammar reference: Questions, page 86

What do you say?

Ss are now going to focus on dealing with questions, particularly problematic questions. Ss work with books closed. Write on the board: *Problems when dealing with questions* and elicit potential problems, e.g. you did not hear the question, you do not know the answer. Write the problems on the board and ask Ss to think of ways of dealing with and / or responding to each problem? Try to cover those points listed on page 68. Then Ss look at page 68 and match each match the problem with a response. Give feedback and ensure Ss practise saying the phrases correctly.

| 1 e | 2 d | 3 a | 4 c | 5 f | 6 b |

[icon] Skills book, Good business practice, Presentations, Dealing with questions, page 77

Culture at work

Before the lesson, write the items from the table on page 69 on separate cards or pieces of paper. Ss work with books closed. Introduce the concept that critical questions can be insulting in some countries. Give out a set of cards to each small group of Ss. Ask Ss to group into the cards into two sets: *Criticism is acceptable* and *Criticism is insulting*. Ss look at the table on page 69 to check their answers. Elicit any reactions / experiences and generate a discussion. Ask the Ss about where they think their own culture fits. Then ask Ss to complete their own culture profile about attitudes to critical questions on page 82. (Ss identify and mark with a cross where they believe their culture is situated on the line ranging from Criticism is acceptable to Criticism is insulting.) Ask Ss how they would deal with questions in presentations when doing business with a culture that is different in this respect? One option is to ask questions in private rather than at a public presentation. Another option is to ask open questions that allow the presenter to respond in the level of detail that he / she feels appropriate.

Skills book, Culture profile, page 82

Task 3

Ss now have the opportunity to put everything together, using strategies and language for asking and dealing with questions. Ss work in the same pairs as for Task 1. Ask each S to read the appropriate additional information on pages 99 and 101. Ss then ask and answer the questions prepared in Task 2, using the additional information. Monitor and take notes for feedback.

Analysis, Task 3

Allow Ss a few minutes to reflect on the questions individually, then start a group discussion.

Self-assessment

Allow Ss a few minutes to think about what they have achieved from the unit and tick the boxes. Suggest what Ss can do to gain further practice.

Video, Part 5

CD-Rom

Unit 15: Celebrate success

UNIT OBJECTIVES	
Skills:	Conclude a deal
	Review achievement
	Celebrate the conclusion
Language:	Past modals
Culture at work:	Giving praise

This activity integrates practice of language to celebrate a deal (following a successful negotiation) with practice of language for saying goodbye at the end of the course. If you do not plan to use it in one of the final lessons of the course, you may wish to adapt some of the activities.

At the end of a deal, it is useful to consider the following:
- Summarising what has been agreed to avoid any misunderstanding
- Signing the agreement
- Celebrating closure of the deal.

Cultural attitudes may have an impact on:
- whether a written summary / agreement is needed in addition to or in place of a verbal agreement
- the idea of what a celebration entails, e.g. some people will drink champagne; some people do not drink alcohol
- whether a toast of thanks or good wishes is commonplace and its level of formality
- the location of the celebration, e.g. in the workplace or in a business associate's home
- the form of farewell, e.g. shaking hands, bowing.

(Negotiating skills were introduced in Unit 11. You may choose to use the negotiation practice from this unit without working through the complete unit.)

Skills book, Unit 11, page 52

Teacher's book, page 157

Task 1

Introduce the topic of the lesson: celebrating success. In fact, this lesson focuses on two types of success: success in a deal and success at the end of a course. The first part of the lesson will focus on success in a deal. In order to be able to celebrate, one needs to have concluded a deal successfully. Ss have the chance to do this in Task 1. The idea is for Ss to be able to reach a position where they can use one of the phrases on page 70. Ask Ss to look at both situations. They will work in groups of four. Two Ss will negotiate a deal for Situation 1, observed by the other two Ss. They will then exchange roles for Situation 2. Point out what the observers should be looking for when observing the negotiations.

Situation 1: Check that Ss understand key vocabulary in Situation 1 and teach additional vocabulary that you think may be useful, e.g. *product life span, fixed price, fee, lump sum, income from sales, share of profits, royalties*. Check that Ss realise that K stands for thousand, i.e. €200K = €200,000 and that if they break down the figures, we are talking about a profit per unit sold of €20. Ss have only a short time to prepare. Nevertheless, remind them that when negotiating, they need to think about their overall objectives first and to break these down into potential 'negotiables', i.e. items they can negotiate over to make up the whole package. Once they have identified possible negotiables, they need to think of what this means in terms of what they will ask for and what they will accept. Ss can negotiate a combination of options – or any other solution they find appropriate. Ss role-play in pairs, observed by the other Ss in their group. Take notes yourself so that you can also give feedback later in Task 2.

Situation 2: Check that Ss understand key vocabulary in Situation 2 and teach additional vocabulary that you think may be useful. Check that Ss realise if they break down the figures, we could be talking about the following: 30 hours = €9,000, 45 hours = €13,500, 50 hours = €15,000 – but the company has a budget of only €12,000. Ensure that Ss are aware that if the consultant is paid on the basis of hours worked only, a large number of hours may be accumulated but the work done may not be what the company wants. Ss may therefore want to consider an agreement also based on deliverables (i.e. achievement of concrete items which are 'delivered'). The procedure for the negotiation is as above.

Before Ss start the negotiation, you may wish to review the use of gerunds in negotiations (see Language focus on the next page)

> There are no correct answers. The objective is to reach a deal which is acceptable to both parties.

> **Optional activity**
> **Photocopiable resource 15.1 (page 184)**
> You may want to extend the planning phase of the negotiation. If so, give each S a copy of the negotiation planning sheet. Ss work in small groups (As together and Bs together) to plan. Ss make notes on the sheet to help them focus on what they are aiming to achieve, what they think their partner may be aiming to achieve, and also some useful phrases.

> **Use of the gerund in negotiations**
>
> We use the gerund after prepositions and following certain verbs. The gerund is used in the following aspects of negotiations.
>
> **Asking questions**
> *How much are you thinking **of charging**?*
> *Would you **consider accepting** a lower figure?*
>
> **Making proposals**
> *We **suggest fixing** a flat rate.*
>
> **Pointing out benefits**
> *That way, we could save money **by ordering** less frequently.*
> *That'd **mean making** fewer deliveries.*

Task 2

Explain that the observers are now going to give their feedback verbally. To do so, refer Ss to the phrases on page 71 and elicit other phrases for giving feedback about past events. Encourage Ss to give constructive feedback and draw their attention to the effect of saying *you might have / you could have* as opposed to *you should have* (see Language focus below). Review the use and form of past modals and Conditional 3 if necessary. Ask observers to give feedback in small groups to those they observed. Then ask observers to summarise for the whole class. Ask each observer to report their three most important pieces of feedback. Give feedback on the observers' use of language.

> **Language focus: Giving feedback**
>
> We often use past modal forms or Conditional 3 when reviewing achievement or giving feedback (praise or criticism):
> *You shouldn't have said exactly what you were prepared to accept at such an early stage in the negotiation.*
> *If you'd tried to look at things from their point of view too, you would have been able to reach an agreement more quickly.*
>
> However, we can sound very negative when we use *should*. It is often more constructive to use *might* or *could*.
> *It **might** have been better to ask more questions in order to find out what was important to the other party.*
> *Perhaps you **could** have been more flexible.*

Skills book, Grammar reference: Conditional type 3 and past modal forms, page 90

Culture at work

Ask Ss for instances of when they received praise, in a work or non-work situation, or of when someone they know received praise. What achievement was praised? Was praise given to the person alone, or to the whole class / team / department? How was the praise given? Verbally / in writing / through a financial reward? How did they feel when praised (e.g. pleased or embarrassed)? How do they think the other people involved felt? Refer Ss to page 71. Can Ss relate to one side of the table, or to a mixture? Have Ss experience of any cultures different from their own in this respect? How did this make them feel? Then ask Ss to complete their own culture profile about giving praise on page 82. (Ss identify and mark with a cross where they believe their culture is situated on the line ranging from Individual praise to Group praise. You may wish to ask Ss to write two marks on the line: a cross indicating their company culture, and a circle indicating the culture in general in their country.)

Skills book, Culture profile, page 82

What do you think? **1** **2**

A lot of attention tends to be given to planning and the earlier stages of a deal. It is also important to ensure that the deal is concluded well. All parties need to be clear what has been agreed and what needs to be done before any celebrations start. Refer Ss to page 72. Ss individually read the list and tick the things in the appropriate boxes. Open up to a group discussion.

> There are no particular right or wrong answers; practice may vary according to culture. Normally, however, it is important to do the following before any celebrations start in order to ensure that the deal has been firmly concluded:
> - Summarise verbally to ensure that any misunderstandings are identified before proceeding to the next stage
> - Prepare a written version of what has been agreed for both parties to agree on (this does not need to in the form of minutes; nor does it need to be a legal agreement yet; the purpose is to check agreement before proceeding to a legal agreement)
> - Both parties sign a formal agreement.

UNIT 15

📘 Skills book, Good business practice, Negotiating, Concluding a negotiation, page 81

Listening

Ss are now going to listen to the end of a negotiation similar to the first situation in Task 1. Ss read the scenario on page 72. Before Ss look at the questions, ask them to listen globally and to notice anything that suggests the deal was successful (language such as *excellent, we've agreed, that sounds really good*). Then ask Ss to listen a second time and to note down what has actually been agreed. *What does Jon agree to do? What does Daniel's company agree to do? What are the benefits for Jon? And the benefits for Daniel's company?* Ss then read the questions on page 72 and listen again to answer them. Elicit Ss' answers and give feedback. Elicit any other ways Ss know to express pleasure at a successful deal and to refer to future business relations. Ensure Ss are comfortable with the pronunciation and grammatical forms of such phrases.

> a The agreement is summarised verbally first. (The parties are ready to celebrate at this point.) The agreement will be finalised in writing and a copy will be sent to Jon by courier as soon as possible. The agreement will then be signed by both parties at a meeting next week.
> b By going to a restaurant and drinking champagne
> c Jon: I'd just like to say that I'm really pleased we've got a deal, and I think the venture is going to be a great success for both of us.
> Daniel: We're very pleased to be working with you. I'm sure we're going to have a long and profitable relationship!

What do you say?

Now that a successful deal has been concluded, Ss may need to know phrases to thank, praise, show appreciation, toast and offer good wishes. Ss match each function with two phrases. Give feedback, ensuring Ss are happy with the pronunciation of the phrases. You may need to practise the intonation to ensure the correct positive message is communicated. Sounding positive normally involves intonation that falls from a peak on the final main stressed syllable; the speaker can sound more positive by pushing the peak higher before the intonation falls.

> 1 f g   2 a e   3 b c   4 d i   5 h j

Task 3

This activity integrates practice of language to celebrate a deal with practice of language for saying goodbye at the end of the course. The focus now shifts to Ss expressing their own thoughts at the end of their course.

Part 1: Ensure that Ss know the collocation *to propose a toast*. Remind Ss of the language for proposing a toast from the previous exercise (*I'd like to propose a toast to ...* or *Here's to ...*). Ss work individually and prepare a toast to something appropriate at the end of the course. Ss check what they have prepared with a partner. If appropriate, supply Ss with glasses (e.g. filled with water) and set an example by proposing the first toast, e.g. *Here's to everyone in this class. I've enjoyed working with you all and wish you the very best as you return to work and continue using English.* Ss then take turns to stand up and propose their toasts. Welcome the sentiments of the toast and perhaps discreetly reformulate what Ss say, if necessary – but do not focus on correction at this stage.

Part 2: Provide a model of saying goodbye divided into three stages. Suggest that Ss might want to add extra details at stage 2, as in the following example.

1 Say goodbye: *Well, goodbye, Peter.*

2 Say something positive about the past or present: *It's been really great working with you. I've particularly enjoyed watching you take part so enthusiastically in role-plays and simulations.*

3 Make reference to the future: *I hope everything goes really well for you when you start your new job.*

Encourage Ss to address everyone in the class. However, if it is difficult to walk around the room, Ss may find it easier to turn in their seats and speak to those nearest. At the end of the activity, do not focus on correction. Instead, give your best wishes for Ss' future and for their future English studies. You may wish to suggest how Ss can continue learning.

Self-assessment

Allow Ss a few minutes to think about what they have achieved from the unit and tick the boxes. Suggest what Ss can do to gain further practice.

📘 Teacher's book, Negotiation planner, page 184
📘 Video, Part 5
📘 CD-Rom

INTELLIGENT BUSINESS (INTERMEDIATE) TEACHER'S BOOK: SKILLS BOOK

Writing 5: Minutes

UNIT OBJECTIVES	
Skills:	Start and end minutes
	Record decisions and action points
Language:	Passives

Minutes are a written record of a meeting. They usually record when the meeting took place, who attended, what was discussed and what the outcomes were (decisions and action points). However, the format of minutes can vary and some organisations and cultures treat them more formally than others. The following may be important when writing minutes:

- The reader (What is their relationship to the writer? What is their level of knowledge of the subject and their level of English?)
- The purpose of the minutes (Do they need to be a comprehensive summary in order to inform people who were unable to attend the meeting? Are they an official record of the meeting? Or are they simply a reminder of points for action?)
- The structure of the minutes (use of headings, numbered points etc.)
- Clarity, conciseness, consistency
- The level of formality
- Accuracy (grammar, spelling, punctuation).

Cultural attitudes (varying according to national culture and also organisational culture) may have an impact on the following:

- Use of minutes
- Length of the minutes
- Speed with which minutes are produced and circulated after the meeting
- Formality of language and procedure.

Style guide, Minutes, page 24
Teacher's book, Writing preparation framework, page 188
Teacher's book, Writing feedback framework, page 189
Teacher's book, page 49 and 142

What do you think?

Introduce the topic of the session: writing minutes (formal and informal). Start by brainstorming the purpose of minutes and collate ideas on the board. Key ideas may include: to record when the meeting took place, who attended, what was discussed and what the outcomes were (decisions and action points). Ask Ss whether they often use minutes themselves, and if so, are they generally formal or less formal? If Ss are not familiar with minutes, you may wish to show some examples that you have collected before the lesson. Ensure there are examples of formal and informal minutes. Refer Ss to page 74 and explain the layout. The page shows four stages of the minutes of a meeting (headlines, who was at the meeting, first agenda point, ending). Within each stage there is a formal and an informal example, each identified by a box. Ss decide which example in each pair is formal (F) and which is informal (I) and write F or I in the box. During feedback, ask Ss to provide specific examples of formal and informal style.

Headlines: First example I. Second example F.

Who was at the meeting: First example I. Second example F (Names and titles of those present are given. The names of people unable to attend are introduced using the typical formal phrase *Apologies were received from* ...).

First agenda point: First example F (The minutes of the previous meeting were officially approved. The meeting has an official Chair). Second example I.

Ending: First example I (The style of the minutes is brief and almost note form. Action is listed using the following note form: *JD to send a memo before the next meeting.*) Second example F (The passive and formal language, e.g. *enquired*, are used).

What do you write? 1

Explain that a key function of minutes is to record decisions and action points. Refer Ss to the two extracts which record decisions and action points about the same situation. Check Ss understand the situation. Ask Ss to underline the words in the formal version that are omitted in the informal one and to notice the difference between the two versions. Give feedback. Since Ss may well have to write both styles of minutes, they need to feel confident using passives. Review the use and form of passives, referring Ss to page 91. (See also Language focus on the next page.)

WRITING 5

The two versions are each divided into three sections:
1 title, 2 decision, 3 action.

1 The titles are written slightly differently.
2 In the part where the decision is recorded, the underlined words are omitted in the informal version:

<u>As</u> our existing stationery supplier can no longer deliver in our area, <u>it was agreed that we</u> need to identify a new supplier before <u>the</u> end of January.

- The informal version:
  uses short sentences instead of longer sentences with linking words
- omits the passive to describe what was agreed
- uses a type of note form, omitting articles (*the*).

3 In the part where action is recorded, three separate bits of information from the formal minutes are combined in one short phrase. The formal version uses the passive (*A decision will be taken at the next meeting*) whereas the informal version uses a short simple phrase (*Duncan to get three quotes by 20th*). NB: This short phrase includes three important pieces of information about the action to be taken: What action? Who will take it? When by?

Skills book, Grammar reference, Passives, page 91

Language focus:
Passives in formal minutes of meeting

The passive is often used in formal minutes of meetings. This is because the decision of the meeting and the consensus of the group are more important than who said what.
Details of proposed trips will be recorded in future.

It is common to avoid reporting personal opinions by using an impersonal style with phrases starting *It was ... It was felt / agreed / proposed that ...*

If the person doing the action is important, this is usually recorded using *by*. It is particularly important to record names when minuting action to be taken.
The budget will be revised by Roger Atwood.

What do you write? 2

Ss are now going to record some decisions and action points. Ask Ss to read the extract from the minutes. Check comprehension by asking questions. Divide the class into two and ask one half to write in a formal style the action points for 2.2 of the minutes and to write in an informal style the action points for 2.3. The other half of the class do the opposite. Monitor and give feedback, recording any useful points on the board under two headings: *Formal* and *Informal*. You may also want to refer Ss to additional differences between formal and informal writing pointed out in page 142 of the Teacher's book for Writing 2.

Suggested answer
2.2 Travel budget (formal)
In order to plan more effectively, it was agreed that details of proposed business trips would be sent to Maria to be charted and the budget for the final quarter would then be revised by Roger.
Action: Project team members, Maria, Roger
Deadline: 25 September
2.2 Travel budget (informal)
Action:
Details of business trips to be sent to Maria. Maria to chart business trip details. Roger to revise budget for final quarter by 25 September
2.3 Training (formal)
It was agreed that those who have attended training should write a short report on their experience and distribute it to other team members. It was decided that Isabel should be responsible for reminding staff to prepare and distribute their reports.
Action: All staff attending training, Isabel
2.3 Training (informal)
Action: All staff to write short report on training attended. Isabel to remind staff to prepare and distribute reports.

Task 1

Ss now have the chance to write some minutes themselves. They should aim to use the ideas introduced on the last two pages. If Ss did the mini meetings in Unit 13, Ss should write the minutes to those. (You will need to refresh their memories by turning to Task 3 on page 65 and eliciting decisions taken.) If they cannot remember, or did not take part in those meetings, Ss may devise their own scenario, or write minutes for an actual meeting they have attended. Weaker Ss may wish to work in pairs. Ask Ss to show their writing to the other Ss for peer correction. If computers and a projector are available, Ss should type their minutes using a computer. Alternatively, ask Ss to write their minutes for homework. Give your feedback on the Ss' writing. You may want to use the Writing preparation framework and the Writing feedback framework on pages 188 and 189.

Skills book, Unit 13, page 65

Photocopiable resource 1.1: Card activity (talking about your job)

Company: Medi4us (pharmaceutical company) **Job:** Sales rep (involves visiting hospitals and doctors' surgeries, promoting new drugs) **Current activities:** Discussing new migraine tablets with the Ministry of Health	**Company:** WiseInsure (insurance company) **Job:** Head of HR (involves recruitment, appraisals, staff discipline and development) **Current activities:** Developing and testing a new appraisal system	**Company:** Speeditrans (distribution company) **Job:** Secretary (responsible for dealing with post [internal and external], answering the telephone, receiving visitors) **Current activities:** Organising a conference for overseas clients
Company: Merlon Printing **Job:** Security guard (involves checking the warehouse is secure at night, monitoring people entering and leaving the premises) **Current activities:** Introducing an electronic card entry system	**Company:** Computing Consult plc **Job:** Trainer (responsible for running IT training courses to external companies) **Current activities:** Producing an online course to support face-to-face seminars	**Company:** Xpo Bank **Job:** Branch Manager (contact with head office, in charge of 30 staff, responsible for customer satisfaction) **Current activities:** Doing a client survey (face-to-face and online)

Photocopiable resource 1.2: Card activity (present tenses)

Set 1

Regular events	Facts	Events happening now	Temporary situations
They're not attending this meeting.	Are you enjoying this seminar?	I don't work in a team.	How often do you visit your clients?
My company provides financial advice to clients.	We're working on a project to improve customer relations.	We meet every Tuesday.	Are you offering discounts this month?
I'm working at Head Office this week.	They don't usually reply to emails straight away.	He's not travelling so much while his health's not good.	Who does she report to?

Set 2

Verbs of opinion / feeling	Verbs of the senses	Verbs of ownership
taste	understand	prefer
want	belong	like
think	mean	smell
hear	feel	
see	have	

Photocopiable resource 2.1: Planning for a deadline

Task:	**Deadline:**

1

2

3

4

5

Photocopiable resource 4.1: Present perfect / past simple questionnaire

What and when?

1 Have you ever attended an international meeting?
   - If so, when did you attend it?
   - Where was it?
   - Did you notice any cultural differences? Give details.

2 Have you ever worked with someone from a different culture (a client, a colleague, a supplier etc.)?
   - If so, when did you work with them?
   - Who was it with?
   - Did you notice any cultural differences? Give details.

3 Have you ever met someone from a different culture in a social situation (on holiday, in a restaurant, at the airport etc.)?
   - If so, when did you meet them?
   - Where did you meet them?
   - Did you notice any cultural differences? Give details.

Photocopiable resource 6.1: Card activity (comparatives and superlatives)

Giving a presentation isn't as easy	than a BMW 6.	Renting offices in the suburbs is cheaper	as talking to friends.
Although this mobile phone is small, it is heavier	than today.	A Renault Clio is less powerful	expensive models are not always the best.
Planning ahead is more effective	the heaviest?	We hope that the weather will be better	largest share of the market.
Which model is	than the other model.	The most	option available to us.
This is the best	than being in the city centre.	This chart shows that camera phones have the	than trouble-shooting.

Photocopiable resource 7.1: Tentative suggestions

Tentative suggestions:

1. if / we / invest / more in advertising / we / increase / sales
2. it / be / a good idea / if / you / not / mention / your concerns
3. what if / we / reconsider / the price?
4. perhaps / we / wait / for your colleague to return
5. one possibility / be / bring forward / the delivery date
6. I / not / suppose / I / discuss / the idea / with my team first?
7. they / accept / the offer / if / you / deliver / free of charge
8. we / be / able to / start / work / straight away / if / we / agree / on / a letter of intent

PHOTOCOPIABLE © Pearson Education Limited 2005

INTELLIGENT BUSINESS (INTERMEDIATE) TEACHER'S BOOK: SKILLS BOOK

Photocopiable resource 8.1: Card activity (language of change)

to increase	to rise	to fall	to decrease
to go up	to drop	an increase	a rise
a fall	a decrease	a drop	sharply
slightly	steadily	to stay at the same level	sudden
dramatic	to fluctuate	a fluctuation	gradual
sharp	slight	steady	to remain constant
suddenly	dramatically	gradually	

Photocopiable resource 9.1: Domino card activity (questions)

your company export?	Where do you	about your staff?	How
you?	Do you mind	live?	And
isn't it?	How long	have you worked for IBM?	You'll give my regards
to Sue, won't you?	Would you	if I ask what the standard of living is like?	It's an interesting conference
mind if I spoke to your boss?	What	did you get here?	Does

Photocopiable resource 9.2: Card activity (socialising)

Situation 1: A
- You only just made it to the meeting in time yourself – traffic was terrible.
- You'd like to be able to travel by train but it's not convenient.
- You have to take the children to school before coming to work.

Situation 2: A
- You like the look of the restaurant – it is light and modern.
- You haven't been before.
- You are impressed with the choice on the menu – you've chosen salmon.

Situation 3: A
- You think the meeting was very productive.
- You hope the finance department agrees to the budget.
- You have a tram to catch in a few minutes.

Situation 1: B
- You came by train this morning – there were no problems.
- You like travelling by train as you can read or do some work.
- Your children are older and have left home.

Situation 2: B
- You find the staff at the restaurant very helpful.
- You've been before – you came a few months ago.
- The menu has been changed since you last came – they now do more fish dishes.

Situation 3: B
- You feel everyone contributed to the meeting.
- You are confident the budget is fine.
- Your friend is collecting you as you are going out this evening.

Photocopiable resource 11.1: Card activity (gerund or infinitive)

Gerund	Infinitive	before	after	without
look forward to	it's no good	consider	postpone	risk
suggest	it's easy	it's important	agree	aim
decide	advise	like	prefer	recommend
remember	avoid	afford	promise	how about

INTELLIGENT BUSINESS (INTERMEDIATE) TEACHER'S BOOK: SKILLS BOOK

Photocopiable resource 13.1: Card activity (reported speech)

Jacques stressed the importance of good design.	"I can't emphasise enough how important good design is."	Gina raised the question of reliability.	"Could you possibly let us have your comments?"
Tina suggested mailing all the customers.	"Yes, we need to offer more training." "I'd go along with that." "Me too."	The technical department warned us to use safety procedures.	"Have you thought about the fact that employing a local workforce will be expensive."
Hannah promised to keep everyone informed.	"I'll let you all know what the developments are."	"Just how reliable is it?"	"If you don't use the specified safety procedures, you'll be liable for damage."
The Board has asked us to report back with our comments.	We've considered postponing the project.	We've agreed to hold monthly meetings.	"How about putting the project back to the autumn?" "Hmmm, it might solve the issue – we need to get some more facts before we decide."
Mr Jackson pointed out that local labour would be expensive.	"How about mailing all the customers?"	Everyone agreed that more training was needed.	"OK, motion passed – our meetings will now take place every month."

Photocopiable resource 13.2: Card activity (meeting)

You have lots of ideas but they're not on the agenda. Digress and talk about something else.	You can't wait for everyone to finish speaking. Interrupt everyone at least once.	You're not very good at saying what you mean. Speak in a complicated way.	You don't have much to say.

Photocopiable resource 14.1: Questions following a presentation

Link to presentation	+	Request for information
Quotation e.g. You say that 1 2		**Question** Can you give us ..., please?
Comment about what was said	+	**Question**
e.g. ... is going to be risky. 1 2		Can you please explain how the company is going to ...?
So, ...	+	**Question**
e.g. So, 1 2		why did the company decide to ...?
Polite general question	+	**Specific question**
e.g. Would you mind telling us a bit more about ...? 1 2		Where exactly ...?

Photocopiable resource 15.1: Negotiation planner

	Objectives	Negotiables	Proposal	Minimum acceptable	Deal agreed
My planning					
What the other party may plan					
Useful phrases	If you…, then I could accept … Provided you …, then I … I can agree to … on the understanding that you …				

PHOTOCOPIABLE FRAMEWORKS

Frameworks

Seven photocopiable framework sheets are provided for task preparation and feedback.

1. **Presentation preparation framework**
   Give a photocopy of the framework to Ss when they are preparing for a longer presentation. The first section focuses the presenter on the audience and the purpose of the presentation. The second section encourages the presenter to plan a clear structure and to think of key language. The final section provides space to note down additional useful phrases.

2. **Presentation feedback framework**
   This framework may be used by teachers giving feedback on Ss, and also by Ss giving peer feedback. It acts as a reminder that accuracy is not the key feature of a presentation in a second language; clear structure and signposting, and interesting content and delivery are often more important.

3. **Writing preparation framework**
   This framework helps Ss to structure and plan their writing. It is particularly useful for the Write it up section of the Dilemma at the end of each Coursebook unit. The Teacher's notes for the Dilemma guide you through the framework in relation to a particular genre and refer you to the relevant pages of the Style guide.

4. **Writing feedback framework**
   This framework may also be used to give feedback from the teacher or from peers. Once again, it reminds those giving feedback that accuracy is one element of communication only; clear structure, arguments and layout, and clear and appropriate language are equally important.

5. **Skills feedback framework**
   This framework is similar to the presentation feedback above – but usable in a greater range of situations. Circle the skill practised (e.g. telephoning).

6. **Accuracy feedback sheet**
   Use this sheet to give feedback following a variety of tasks. Accuracy feedback can relate to vocabulary and pronunciation as well as grammar. Start with specific positive feedback. Then focus on error correction. Finally, encourage Ss to focus on what is achievable. If Ss are too ambitious, they are likely to fail; therefore, ask them to monitor no more than three language points. When they feel confident, they can tick off these points and identify three more specific areas for improvement.

7. **Vocabulary record sheet**
   Remind Ss that noting down a word means more than just recording its meaning. This sheet has three frameworks for Ss to record vocabulary. The first is a standard word diagram (or spider diagram) usable for recording vocabulary related to a central concept. It is also usable to indicate collocations in relation to the central word. In the final framework, Ss write a vocabulary item in the centre and different information about the item in each petal, e.g. petal 1 = meaning, petal 2 = pronunciation, petal 3 = formal / informal, petal 4 = other comments.

Presentation preparation framework

Student:		Date:
Title of presentation:		

Who is my presentation aimed at?	
What am I trying to achieve in my presentation?	

Stage	Key points	Key language
Introduction		
Body		
Conclusion		

Signposting and linking phrases	
Phrases for referring to visuals	

Presentation feedback framework

Student: **Date:**

Title of presentation:

Content
- Purpose?
- Interest?
- Appropriateness?

Structure
- Structure?
- Organisation?
- Signposting?
- Linking?

Grammar
- Accuracy?
- Appropriateness?

Vocabulary
- Accuracy?
- Appropriateness?
- Pronunciation?

Delivery
- Pronunciation?
- Chunking?
- Projection?
- Eye contact?
- Body language?
- Communication?

Other comments

Writing preparation framework

Student:		**Date:**
Lesson focus:		

Type of writing e.g. formal / informal letter / report / memo?	
Who am I writing from?	
Purpose	
Target reader	
Structure and organisation • Is there a typical structure and layout that I can follow? • What sections should I divide my document into? • What can I do to ensure layout supports my message?	
Style • Formal / informal / neutral style? • Tone?	
Useful phrases	
Checks Have I checked my writing for: • logical structure? • clarity of ideas? • accuracy of language?	

Writing feedback framework

Student:		Date:
Lesson focus:		

Planning • Clarity of purpose? • Achievement of objectives? • Appropriateness for target reader?	
Layout • Appropriatenes of layout? e.g. formal / informal letter / report / memo • Clarity of layout? (paragraphs, headings, white space, bullets)	
Organisation and clarity • Clear points? • Organisation? • Support for main points? • Sentence length? • Conciseness? • Linking of ideas?	
Language • Accuracy? • Range? • Appropriateness? (formality / tone)	
Other comments	

Skills feedback framework

Student:		**Date:**
Skill (*circle as appropriate*): Socialising / Meeting / Negotiating / Telephoning Other (*please specify*)		

Communication • Task achievement? • Comprehension? • Responding? • Checking and clarifying? • Showing interest? • Turn-taking? • Fluency? • Effectiveness?	
Pronunciation • Sounds? • Stress and intonation? • Chunking?	
Grammar • Accuracy? • Range? • Appropriateness?	
Vocabulary • Accuracy? • Range? • Appropriateness?	
Other comments • Cultural awareness?	

Accuracy feedback sheet

Student:		Date:
Lesson focus:		

What you did well

What you did less well

What you said / wrote	What you should have said / written

Action plan

List no more than three specific points (identified on this feedback sheet) that you are going to focus on and monitor when speaking and writing

1

2

3

INTELLIGENT BUSINESS (INTERMEDIATE) TEACHER'S BOOK

Vocabulary record sheet

Student: **Date:**

Lesson focus:

- Use some or all of the ways suggested below to record key vocabulary.
- Remenber that knowing a word or phrase is more than just knowing its meaning.

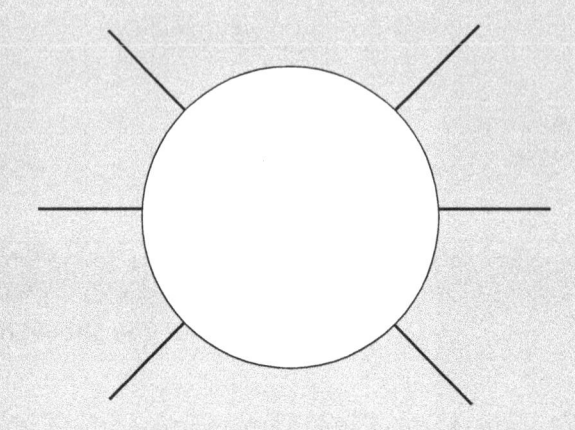

Noun	Verb	Adjective	Adverb

© Pearson Education Limited 2005   PHOTOCOPIABLE